# GRACE CULTURE

## TRANSFORMED BY THE LOVE OF JESUS

## D.A. HORTON

Lifeway Press®
Brentwood, Tennessee

ISBN 978-1-0877-7602-6

Item 005839872

Dewey Decimal Classification Number: 242

Subject Heading: DEVOTIONAL LITERATURE / BIBLE STUDY AND TEACHING / GOD

Printed in the United States of America.

Student Ministry Publishing

Lifeway Resources

200 Powell Place, Suite 100,
Brentwood, TN 37027

We believe that the Bible has God for its author; salvation for its end; truth, without any mixture of error, for its matter; and that all Scripture is totally true and trustworthy. To review Lifeway's doctrinal guideline, please visit www.lifeway.com/doctrinalguideline.

# PUBLISHING TEAM

**DIRECTOR, STUDENT MINISTRY**

Ben Trueblood

**MANAGER, STUDENT MINISTRY PUBLISHING**

John Paul Basham

**EDITORIAL TEAM LEADER**

Karen Daniel

**CONTENT EDITOR**

Kyle Wiltshire

**PRODUCTION EDITOR**

Stephanie Cross

**GRAPHIC DESIGNER**

Shiloh Stufflebeam

# TABLE OF CONTENTS

About the Author                                      4

Intro                                                 5

How to Use this Bible Study                           6

How to Access Videos                                  7

Session 1: The Power of Stories                       8

Session 2: The Necessity of Discipleship             22

Session 3: The Messiness of Discipleship             36

Session 4: Creating Grace Culture                    50

Session 5: Abiding in Jesus                          64

Session 6: The Day to Day                            78

Leader Helps                                         92

Sources                                              95

# ABOUT THE AUTHOR

D.A. Horton, PhD, serves as an Assistant Professor and Program Director of Intercultural Studies at California Baptist University. He is blessed to also serve as an Associate Teaching Pastor at The Grove Community Church in Riverside, CA. He earned his BS in Biblical Studies and his MS in Christian Studies from Calvary Theological Seminary and his PhD in Applied Theology with a North American Missions emphasis at Southeastern Baptist Theological Seminary. He and his wife, Elicia, have been married for twenty years, and have been blessed by God with two daughters and one son.

# INTRO

Every neighborhood, school, and even church you visit has a unique culture. What I mean by culture is a vibe, a feeling, an understanding of how things work and flow. Sometimes the culture in these places is fun, friendly, and positive; sometimes it's not. Today we live in a culture that likes to project itself as fun, friendly, and positive, but at it's root, it's anything but. Don't believe me? Just mess up and see what happens. See how fast you get canceled from this current culture as soon as you do something that whichever group in power doesn't like or agree with. To be canceled means to be kicked out from influence, invalidated, and shamed. It's a tough place to be.

This is why we are in such desperate need of grace culture. Grace culture occurs when forgiveness, accountability, and love are truly at the center of everything. It's the culture Jesus set up with His disciples so many years ago, and the one He wants the church to display and carry to a lost and dying world. Grace culture requires patience, understanding, and a willingness to "go there" with people. Everyone will make mistakes, but how we respond when someone fails defines what kind of culture we have created.

This book is a guide to help you build a culture of grace in your community. Grace culture doesn't turn a blind eye to sin—just the opposite. Grace culture helps us come back when we have sinned. It doesn't leave us abandoned, alone, depressed, and desperate. Nether does our heavenly Father. God never leaves us or kicks us out of the family. He deals with us in grace, and we should deal with each other the same way.

I'm excited for you to begin this journey. So, let's get started.

# HOW TO USE THIS BIBLE STUDY

This Bible study book includes six sessions of content. Each session includes video teaching, followed by content designed to be used by groups and individuals.

## VIDEO

Each teaching video is 10-12 minutes long and is designed to help students think about the topic for the session and engage in discussion. There is a guide with blanks to fill in as students watch the video teaching. Video content can be purchased at lifeway.com/graceculture.

## GROUP DISCUSSION

These pages include teaching, questions, and activities that guide students to respond to the video teaching and to relevant Bible passages. It's important to consider the age, maturity level, and needs of students as you tailor this content for your group.

## PERSONAL STUDY

Three days of personal study are provided for each session to take students deeper into Scripture and to further the biblical truths introduced in the group discussion and teaching time. These pages challenge students to grow in their understanding of God's Word and to make practical applications to their lives.

## LEADER HELPS

At the back of the book is more content to help walk students through the material. There you will find a summary from D.A. Horton and an icebreaker activity.

# HOW TO ACCESS THE VIDEOS

This Bible study has six videos—one for each session.
These videos enhance the content and launch discussion.

**To stream the Grace Culture teen Bible study video teaching sessions, follow these steps:**

1. Purchase the group video bundle at lifeway.com/graceculture.
2. Go to my.lifeway.com/redeem and register or log in to your Lifeway account.
3. Enter the redemption code provided at purchase to gain access to your group-use video license.

Once you've entered your personal redemption code, you can stream the video teaching sessions any time from your Digital Media page on my.lifeway.com or watch them via the Lifeway On Demand app on any TV or mobile device via your Lifeway account.

There's no need to enter your code more than once! To watch your streaming videos, just log in to your Lifeway account at my.lifeway.com or watch using the Lifeway On Demand app.

Scan the QR code below to access videos.

### QUESTIONS? WE HAVE ANSWERS!
Visit support.lifeway.com and search "Video Redemption Code" or call our Tech Support Team at 866.627.8553.

Available in the **Lifeway On Demand** app

Stream on these devices:
Roku tv firetv

App Store    Google Play

SESSION ONE

# THE POWER OF STORIES

**2 CORINTHIANS 5:16-21**

From now on, therefore, we regard no one according to the flesh. Even though we once regarded Christ according to the flesh, we regard him thus no longer. Therefore, if anyone is in Christ, he is a new creation. The old has passed away; behold, the new has come. All this is from God, who through Christ reconciled us to himself and gave us the ministry of reconciliation; that is, in Christ God was reconciling the world to himself, not counting their trespasses against them, and entrusting to us the message of reconciliation. Therefore, we are ambassadors for Christ, God making his appeal through us. We implore you on behalf of Christ, be reconciled to God. For our sake he made him to be sin who knew no sin, so that in him we might become the righteousness of God.

That night, I heard a message that changed my life forever—it was _____ _____.

> "My parents were tired of me chasing the things that I thought were the most valuable things in the world: money, drugs, and anything the street life could offer."

"Therefore, if anyone is in Christ, he is a new creation. The old has passed away; behold, the new has come."
—2 Corinthians 5:17

Everyone is made in the _____
_____ _____.

God has given us:

_____

_____

_____

_____

_____ was introduced.

Sin comes with a penalty and a price. The penalty is _____. The price is the shedding of blood of an _____ _____.

Jesus absorbed the wrath of God on the _____.

We can now be connected with God through Christ because Jesus offers everyone who hears this message and turns from a life of sin _____ _____. That's the gospel.

Conciliation: The removal of animosity, distrust, and _____.

# GROUP DISCUSSION

FOCUS STATEMENT:

## The gospel connects God's story to our story.

Our brains and our bodies naturally react to stories. Studies have shown how the human brain triggers emotional responses when we hear a story.[1] This helps explain why our hearts begin beating faster and why we may feel happy or sad when watching a movie. Stories carry power. Good stories change even lives.

What is a story you love? Why?

The most remarkable story ever told is the one revealed by God to humanity—the Bible. It takes us from creation to the fall to redemption to how it all applies to us. But it's not about us. The main character in God's story is not the reader or the original audience, it's Jesus.

## JESUS'S STORY

Jesus—God in human skin—perfectly obeyed God in every way and took the place of humanity on the cross. He received the punishment that was due to every person who has lived or ever will live. Jesus was tempted and challenged to disobey God, yet He remained faithful. Had Jesus sinned, He wouldn't have been a perfect sacrifice and couldn't have been raised from the dead. Since Jesus rose from the grave, He now offers freedom to people of every ethnicity, culture, class, and gender.

What has been your experience with Jesus up to this point in your life?

Jesus's story is summed up in one word—*gospel*. The gospel announces the good news that God made a way for people to be forgiven of their sins, and in exchange, receive life in Jesus so that we can live with God for all eternity.

We all have a story filled with our own unique life experiences. And the gospel connects God's story to our story.

## MY ORIGIN STORY

On Friday, March 29, 1996, I found myself hiding from the police in my friend's mother's closet. She wouldn't let them in her house without a warrant, so they left. Then she told me in no uncertain terms to leave or she'd turn me in. The week before, I had run away from home. Now, the only thing I could do was go back home and face my family.

The four-block walk seemed like an eternity. When I arrived at my house, my mom, dad, brother, and his wife were all waiting for me. The gravity of the guilt and shame for my actions weighed heavily on me. My family was exhausted from my constant running away from home to pursue life on the streets.

As I sat there seeing my family weep, God removed the scales from my eyes, and I realized how my choices were hurting the people who loved me the most. I reached down into the depths of my soul and shared my heart. With tears streaming down my face, I said, "Today, I realize how much I have hurt you all, and I hate the person I have become." I had to find a way to show them I was serious and wanted to change. I said, "I don't want to keep living this way. I want to ask permission to go to church Sunday night."

When have you found yourself at a point where you wanted to change your lifestyle and choices?

It was Sunday, March 31, 1996, and I had not left my room for the past two days. I thought about how all my meaningful relationships were falling apart. I still wanted to go to church that night. We sat in the front row, and our pastor preached the gospel like always. However, this was the first time in ten years of hearing him preach that it cut me to the heart. I realized I did not know God; I loved my sin; and there was nothing I could do to stop myself from the life I was living. I knew that if there was going to be a change, I needed Jesus to give me the strength to make new life choices that glorified Him and no longer allowed my sin to run my life.

I cried uncontrollably and fell to my knees. I crawled to the bottom of the altar, yelling, "Jesus, I'm sorry. I'm so sorry." Then I felt my pastor's hand on my back. He whispered in my ear, "Welcome home, Damon," and tenderly led me in a prayer in which I confessed I was a sinner; I couldn't save myself; and I wanted Jesus to save me from myself and the wrath I deserved. At that moment, the old Damon died, and the new Damon was given life. That's when my story and Jesus's story connected.

When did your story connect with Jesus's?
If it hasn't yet, what is holding you back?

> **Therefore, if anyone is in Christ, he is a new creation. The old has passed away; behold, the new has come.**
>
> 2 CORINTHIANS 5:17

## A NEW CREATION

Even though my life had changed the night before, on Monday, April 1, 1996, I still lived in the same neighborhood and had to walk the same streets that I did before I gave my life to Jesus. That morning my mom challenged me to read 2 Corinthians 5:16-21. She told me that I was a new creation in the eyes of God.

I read 2 Corinthians 5:16-21 and didn't understand what it meant. I remember wishing I had someone who could explain it to me. Maybe you find yourself in a similar situation. I would like to walk you through this passage with the hope that it gives you clarity, comfort, and conviction.

- **NEW LENS:** In verse 16 the apostle Paul explained how judging people based on the way they looked on the outside was part of the old way of life. For his original audience, this included rejecting Jesus as Messiah because He didn't look like a Savior since He was crucified like a criminal. New life in Jesus means to look at people through a new lens.

- **NEW CREATION:** Verse 17 helps us understand that when we embrace Jesus as Savior, we become new creations. This does not mean we won't face consequences for past mistakes. This means we die to our former way of living; we have new life; and the Holy Spirit influences our decisions moving forward.

- **RECONCILIATION:** In verses 18 and 19, Paul explained that the gift of life we have received through faith in Jesus comes from God alone. We were reconciled to God through Christ. To be reconciled means to have a restored relationship.

Why do we need a reconciled relationship with God?

In Genesis 3, because of Adam and Eve's disobedience to God's direct command, sin and death were introduced into the world. This broke our relationship with God and separated the whole human race from Him. Since then, all people have suffered the consequences of sin and death and need a restored relationship with God.

- **NEW MINISTRY:** Verses 20 and 21 explain that the death and resurrection of Jesus is what can bring the human race into a right relationship with God again. We who have embraced Christ as our Savior are now His ambassadors. This means we are His messengers at home, school, and everywhere else we go. Our mission is to communicate God's desire for all people to be reconciled to Him through Jesus.

## OUR STORIES HAVE POWER

Since the gospel connects God's story to our story and we have embraced Christ who sends us out to be His ambassadors, we must share this story.

The greatest news we have ever heard is what Paul said in 2 Corinthians 5:21—because of what Jesus has done for us, we are righteous in the sight of God. We have a new identity in Jesus. My greatest prayer is for you to realize that although this journey is long, once you have embraced Christ, you are in the family of God. He will never leave you or forsake you (see Heb. 13:5). He is trustworthy, and His Word helps understand just how amazing He is toward His children. You are God's child, and He loves you always.

## LET'S WORK ON TELLING YOUR STORY

What was your life like before you met Jesus?

When did you become convinced of the gospel's truth and embrace Jesus as your Savior?

What has life been like since you placed your faith in Jesus?

As you close this time of discussion with your group, pray for one another as you seek to share your gospel story. Ask for God's help as you extend grace culture to the world around you, where you have been called as ambassadors of reconciliation.

# DAY 1

# PETER THE FISHERMAN

READ LUKE 5:1-11.

*On one occasion, while the crowd was pressing in on him to hear the word of God, he was standing by the lake of Gennesaret, and he saw two boats by the lake, but the fishermen had gone out of them and were washing their nets. Getting into one of the boats, which was Simon's, he asked him to put out a little from the land. And he sat down and taught the people from the boat. And when he had finished speaking, he said to Simon, "Put out into the deep and let down your nets for a catch." And Simon answered, "Master, we toiled all night and took nothing! But at your word I will let down the nets." And when they had done this, they enclosed a large number of fish, and their nets were breaking. They signaled to their partners in the other boat to come and help them. And they came and filled both the boats, so that they began to sink. But when Simon Peter saw it, he fell down at Jesus' knees, saying, "Depart from me, for I am a sinful man, O Lord." For he and all who were with him were astonished at the catch of fish that they had taken, and so also were James and John, sons of Zebedee, who were partners with Simon. And Jesus said to Simon, "Do not be afraid; from now on you will be catching men." And when they had brought their boats to land, they left everything and followed him.*

As you read Luke 5:1-11, did you notice how the crowd was pressing in to see Jesus to the point that He needed to get in Peter's (also called Simon) boat so He could speak to the crowd? Imagine what Peter felt while listening to Jesus teach the people. This passage shows that Peter at least respected Jesus because when Jesus told him to row out to the deep water, Peter did. Peter had just come in from a disappointing night when he caught no fish. Yet, Peter said, "But at your word I will let down the nets" (v. 5). And sure enough, they caught so many fish that the weight of the net began to sink the boat!

When have you reluctantly obeyed Jesus? What did He ask you to do?

Peter noticed how big the catch was and immediately said to Jesus, "Depart from me, for I am a sinful man, O Lord" (v. 8). Peter felt unworthy to be in Jesus's presence. How often do you share this same feeling? It's not always a bad feeling because this understanding helps us see we need to run to Jesus, who is willing to embrace us even when we feel unworthy of His love. The truth is, we are unworthy, but Jesus loves us despite our unworthiness! Peter had no filter and confessed he was a sinner and shouldn't be near someone who was so righteous.

What helps you have confidence to approach Jesus even when you feel like you are unworthy?

I love how Jesus responded to Peter, "Do not be afraid; from now on you will be catching men" (v. 10). Jesus saw what Peter would become even when Peter only saw himself as a fisherman who was far from God. Jesus knows that people who were once far from God and embrace Him are the best people to reach those who are still far from God.

Do you feel like you are unworthy? Do you find it hard to see how God can change your heart and make you new? Do you still feel shame because of past decisions or sinful choices? Be encouraged by Peter's story. Over the next few days, we will read more of Peter's story and see how God worked in his heart until he took his last breath. What God did for Peter, He also desires to do in you.

Close this day in prayer. Confess to God where you have feelings of unworthiness. Ask Him to fill you up with confidence in His love and desire to continually change you and transform your heart.

# DAY 2

# PETER THE FOLLOWER

Here's a hard truth: You will never be perfect as you follow Jesus. However, when you fall short, remember Peter and be encouraged that Jesus will never quit walking with you. Prior to Jesus's crucifixion, Peter boldly proclaimed he would lay down his life for Jesus. Jesus responded by telling Peter he would deny Jesus three times (see John 13:36-38). Peter did just as Jesus said he would. Look at this interaction after the resurrection.

READ JOHN 21:15-19.

*When they had finished breakfast, Jesus said to Simon Peter, "Simon, son of John, do you love me more than these?" He said to him, "Yes, Lord; you know that I love you." He said to him, "Feed my lambs." He said to him a second time, "Simon, son of John, do you love me?" He said to him, "Yes, Lord; you know that I love you." He said to him, "Tend my sheep." He said to him the third time, "Simon, son of John, do you love me?" Peter was grieved because he said to him the third time, "Do you love me?" and he said to him, "Lord, you know everything; you know that I love you." Jesus said to him, "Feed my sheep. Truly, truly, I say to you, when you were young, you used to dress yourself and walk wherever you wanted, but when you are old, you will stretch out your hands, and another will dress you and carry you where you do not want to go." (This he said to show by what kind of death he was to glorify God.) And after saying this he said to him, "Follow me."*

Notice how Jesus asked Peter three times if he loved Him. There is some nuance lost in the Bible's translation from the original language. The first two times Jesus asked if Peter loved Him, He used the Greek word for unconditional love. Peter responded with a Greek word that meant, "I dearly love you." It is possible Peter softened his response because he did not want to overcommit to Jesus as he did before when he boldly proclaimed he would die for Jesus and then denied Him three times instead.

Have you ever overcommitted to Jesus? What happened?

When Jesus asked the third time, He said, "Do you dearly love me?" Jesus's asking the same question three times hurt Peter. He might have thought Jesus doubted his commitment and love; however, Jesus was allowing Peter to reaffirm his love for Jesus once for every time Peter had denied Him.

How has Jesus restored you after a time of failure?

Peter's story reminds us that Jesus loves us perfectly, and when we don't love Him ideally, His love for us covers up all our shortcomings. Look back at verse 18. Jesus was telling Peter that in spite of his failures, Peter would follow Jesus until the end of his life. Don't miss two significant elements in Peter's story.

- Jesus told Peter, "Follow me" (v. 19). In the original language, the way Jesus said these words meant "keep following me." So, no matter how many times Peter may have fallen or failed, Jesus's command was "keep following Me!" Jesus says the same thing to His followers today: In spite of sin or continued struggles with your old way of living, don't believe the lie that God is done with you. Keep following Jesus daily.

- Peter would eventually fulfill his commitment to Jesus and die for Him. Verse 19 revealed that Peter never again rejected Jesus and his death glorified God.

Although we may not die for Jesus under persecution like Peter did, we must make the daily choice to live for Jesus and not deny Him. We should take encouragement from Jesus's words to Peter. No matter how many times we fall into sin or fail, we must keep following Jesus!

Close today in prayer. Thank Jesus for His restorative, unconditional love. Ask Him to encourage you to keep following even when you fail. Never believe the lie that God is done with you!

# DAY 3

# PETER THE FINISHER

As we have witnessed Peter's story as a follower of Jesus unfold, we now arrive at the end. Today, we will read Peter's last documented words and the challenge he gave to his readers to finish our race with Jesus as strongly as possible.

READ 2 PETER 3:17-18.

*You therefore, beloved, knowing this beforehand, take care that you are not carried away with the error of lawless people and lose your own stability. But grow in the grace and knowledge of our Lord and Savior Jesus Christ. To him be the glory both now and to the day of eternity. Amen.*

Let's take a moment to reflect on what we have learned about Peter's story so far. His first encounter with Jesus led him to believe he was unworthy to be embraced as one of Jesus's followers. Yet when Jesus asked Peter to leave his career as a fisherman and follow Him, Peter left his job and went with Jesus. As Jesus's disciple, Peter made many mistakes and fell into sin more than a few times. He even boldly claimed he would be willing to die for Jesus, but instead ended up denying Him three times.

Jesus's unconditional love was revealed by how He restored Peter. Remember, this entire time, Jesus saw who Peter would become, even when Peter failed to see it in himself. Now, we find Peter at the end of his life, finally seeing himself as Jesus has, as one who would finish his race and cross the finish line and fall into the arms of Jesus.

How do you see yourself at this stage in your journey of following Jesus?

Our encouragement comes from seeing how Jesus never quit on Peter and, in spite of his failures, Peter never stopped following Jesus. Peter challenges his readers to not be carried away by the lies we hear in our heads, on social media, and in our broken world. Peter said we can only do this and remain steady as a followers of Jesus through being lifelong learners at the feet of Jesus. This is the process we call discipleship. Discipleship is how we "grow in the grace and knowledge of our Lord and Savior Jesus Christ" (2 Pet. 3:17).

From the time we were very young the world has been trying to disciple us. We learn words and actions that show us how to live a life of sin long before we even know it. So, to grow as disciples of Jesus, we need people who have been following Him longer than us to walk beside us and show us how to read Scripture, pray, and make God's story known to others.

In each box, list the name of a person who has or can walk alongside you in that specific area.

|  | Scripture | Prayer | Gospel Sharing |
|---|---|---|---|
| Person |  |  |  |

Think of it this way:

- You're around people like Peter when he was just the fisherman. They are lost and don't want to be around Jesus because they feel unworthy. Remember how you used to feel this way too?

- You're also around people (maybe in your student ministry or school) who are followers of Jesus but have failed and fallen into sin. They need to be reminded that Jesus still loves them and sees who they will become.

- God has also put people in your life who are following Jesus that are closer to being finishers, so you can follow their example until you cross the finish line, just like Peter!

Close today in prayer. Ask God to show you someone who needs encouragement to embrace Jesus. Ask Him to lead you to other Christ-followers who need to be reminded that God loves them no matter how they've failed. Finally, ask Him to direct you to someone who can walk alongside you and be an example for you to follow.

SESSION TWO

# THE NECESSITY OF DISCIPLESHIP

LUKE 6:43-45

"For no good tree bears bad fruit, nor again does a bad tree bear good fruit, for each tree is known by its own fruit. For figs are not gathered from thornbushes, nor are grapes picked from a bramble bush. The good person out of the good treasure of his heart produces good, and the evil person out of his evil treasure produces evil, for out of the abundance of the heart his mouth speaks."

# VIDEO

When we embrace Christ as Savior, we enter into a new relationship that's called

_____.

Discipleship teaches me how to become _____ for the things that I say and do.

> Remember not the sins of my youth or my transgressions; according to your steadfast love remember me, for the sake of your goodness, O Lord!
>
> —PSALM 25:7

Accountability: We have entered into this relationship with the agreement that we will _____ _____ _____ grow in Jesus.

Judgment: I don't know any context, but I'm arriving at a _____.

Discipleship is one maturing Christian linking his or her life together with an immature Christian to grow in _____ together.

When we embrace Jesus, we literally have all of our sins _____.

That's when I began to recognize, "Lord, I need _____ still."

# GROUP DISCUSSION

## Our words and actions reveal what's in our hearts.

Atelophobia is the fear of imperfection.[2] Do you struggle with atelophobia? Do you struggle to reveal your weaknesses in front of others? Maybe it's because you're afraid people will take this information and tell others or use it against you. This would make you vulnerable and potentially open for someone to take advantage of you. Yet, admitting you don't always have it all together or that you're not okay is very helpful in your walk with Jesus.

What are some situations in life when it's hard to admit weakness?

Admitting weakness is one of the most honest confessions we can make. It may be scary, but it provides freedom from the trap of perfectionism. It shows us areas where we need to find others who are strong to walk with us and lend us their strength. When we embrace Jesus as Lord, the Holy Spirit comes to live inside us. Immediately, He starts transforming our lives from the inside out. The first question we should ask the Holy Spirit is, "In what areas of my life am I weak and You want to transform me?"

## THE FRUIT OF OUR ACTIONS AND WORDS

In Luke 6:43, Jesus said, "For no good tree bears bad fruit, nor again does a bad tree bear good fruit." He used trees and fruit to describe His follower's words and actions. Followers of Jesus are good because they have been made righteous by Jesus. When we embrace Him as Lord, the gospel reminds us that our "goodness" comes only through His righteousness (see 2 Cor. 5:21).

Since God sees us as "good," Jesus's words in Luke 6:43 are a call to examine the motives of our hearts. In Galatians 5:19-21, the apostle Paul identified the rotten fruit those who are not followers of Jesus produce. We must remember that before we embraced Jesus, this was the fruit of our lives as well. This list reminds us how much God has changed our hearts and helps us see the places where we still have room to grow. Take a look at the verses and chart below.

READ GALATIANS 5:19-21.

| Sexual Immorality | all forms of sexual expression outside of God's design |
|---|---|
| Impurity | lustful thoughts and actions, both sexual and non-sexual |
| Sensuality | an unrestrained desire to sin |
| Idolatry | the worship of anyone or thing outside of God |
| Sorcery | witchcraft as well as abusing illegal and prescription mind-altering drugs |
| Enmity | deep internal corruption of the heart expressed as hatred |
| Strife | using words to start arguments and fights with people |
| Jealousy | to obsessively desire what other people have |
| Fits of Anger | losing control of your actions and words when angry |
| Rivalries | unchecked ambition for money, fame, or followers that divides people |
| Dissensions | separating yourself from others because of problems you have with them |
| Divisions | separating yourself from others over differing opinions |
| Envy | jealousy that leads to bitterness |
| Drunkenness | being under the influence of alcohol or other substances |
| Orgies | uncontrolled partying and sexual immorality |

Since you've embraced Jesus as Lord, how has He helped rid your life of bad fruit?

Galatians 5:21 makes it clear that all people who live according to these actions and haven't come to Jesus and confessed their sinfulness will never enter the kingdom of God. These are the people who cannot bear good fruit because they are not seen by God as "good."

As Jesus's followers, this truth should lead us to treat those who don't know Him with compassion because we could not bear good fruit at one time. However, through faith in Jesus, we are justified in God's eyes. To be justified means God has declared us not guilty for all the sins we have committed and ever will commit during our lifetime. God justifies us because of Jesus's perfect life, death, and resurrection—not because of any of our words or works. Every follower of Jesus is now free from the eternal debt and the present slavery that come from sin.

Since we are free from the grip of sin, we enjoy freedom in Christ to witness the Holy Spirit produce good fruit in and through us! Read these verses and examine this list.

READ GALATIANS 5:22-23.

| Love | putting the needs of others before our own |
|---|---|
| Joy | gladness regardless of the circumstances we face |
| Peace | finding contentment in Jesus and living in harmony with others |
| Patience | not being easily angered or frustrated, even when it's tough |
| Kindness | showing compassion and grace through words and actions |
| Goodness | helping people by being generous toward them |
| Faithfulness | having a reputation of being dependable and loyal |
| Gentleness | Being respectful, showing honor, not treating other people harshly |
| Self-Control | mastering our desires and keeping them from mastering us |

How do you grow in the "good" fruit of the Spirit in your walk with Jesus?

God has designed new life in Jesus to be lived alongside other Christians. When we open our lives to our family in Christ and join them in growing in Jesus, we call it discipleship. And discipleship is necessary for our development in Christ.

## THE INTERCONNECTEDNESS OF DISCIPLESHIP

In Luke 6:44, Jesus said, "For figs are not gathered from thornbushes, nor are grapes picked from a bramble bush." This means don't go to a thorn bush if you want a fig or a grape. Before I became a follower of Jesus, no one would come to me for figs or grapes; I was a thornbush and so was my circle of friends. Because of this, whether I was doing anything wrong or not, I was guilty by association. Our reputations are directly connected to the people we associate with.

Why are our reputations important as a followers of Jesus?

Once I cut ties with my old circle of friends, God blessed me with young adult leaders and friends my age who helped me develop a new reputation. This was a huge step in my discipleship process. Discipleship is necessary for our development because it helps give us a new reputation connected to our new life in Christ.

Discipleship is like when we're new to a neighborhood, school, or sports team, and someone more experienced comes alongside us to show us how to navigate the situation. Discipleship happens when a spiritually mature Christian links his or her life with a less mature Christian and they grow in maturity together.

Share an experience you have had with discipleship in your walk with Jesus.

The time we spend living life together is called fellowship. The way we act and talk when together displays our witness. Accountability is when we allow our family in Christ to affirm our character development while pointing out areas where we still need to grow. Discipleship brings together fellowship, our witness, and accountability so our reputation can be protected by those with whom we're growing in Christ.

In Luke 6:45, Jesus said "The good person out of the good treasure of his heart produces good, and the evil person out of his evil treasure produces evil." The good we can produce comes directly from the righteousness of Christ in us. The evil we seek to avoid is there because of the sin nature we are born with (see Ps. 51:5).

> "The good person out of the good treasure of his heart produces good, and the evil person out of his evil treasure produces evil."
> —LUKE 6:45

We were made brand-new people when we heard the gospel, turned from our former ways of living, and embraced Jesus. Now we are to seek discipleship relationships with other followers of Jesus. Doing this will help us build a new reputation in Christ that demonstrates we are not the same as we were before we met Jesus. This is a picture of the necessity of discipleship and grace culture.

As you close this time of discussion with your group, pray for each other as you seek discipleship relationships. Ask Him to help you grow in fellowship and accountability, which will lead to a witness and reputation that honors the Lord.

# SATAN'S FIRST ATTACK

READ GENESIS 3:1-3.

*Now the serpent was more crafty than any other beast of the field that the Lord God had made. He said to the woman, "Did God actually say, 'You shall not eat of any tree in the garden'?" And the woman said to the serpent, "We may eat of the fruit of the trees in the garden, but God said, 'You shall not eat of the fruit of the tree that is in the midst of the garden, neither shall you touch it, lest you die.'"*

In Genesis 3 we find two of Satan's most common and effective attack strategies. Today, we'll explore his first approach. Notice how he started the conversation with Eve in Genesis 3:1: "Did God actually say?" Satan was tempting Eve to question God. He knew what God said to Adam and Eve, and he wanted to intentionally distort God's command. It was true in the beginning and it's still true today—Satan is "crafty." The longer he spoke with Eve the more doubt he was able to plant in her heart and mind.

How does Satan distort what God says today?

Let's see how the doubt Satan stirred up in Eve caused her to go off course.

Compare what God actually said in Genesis 2:16-17 with what Eve said in Genesis 3:3. How are they different?

She added in that God instructed Adam and Eve to not even touch the tree in the middle of the garden. Doubting what God says opens the door for us to potentially add to what God says, which is dangerous (see Deut. 4:2). Reading, studying, and memorizing Scripture—the actual Word of God—is the best way to defend against Satan's first attack in our lives.

Why is it dangerous to add to what God's Word says?

Today, take time to read Hebrews 4:12 and consider how God's Word is true. When we read, study, and memorize Scripture, we set ourselves up to stand against Satan's attacks because God's Word offers truth and help in our times of need. We must trust His Word to keep our guard up and ready for Satan's first attack—enticing us to doubt the truthfulness and effectiveness of Scripture.

Close today in prayer. Ask God to help you be aware of Satan's first attack. When he tempts you to doubt God's Word, ask God to direct your heart to the perfect verses to help you fight the evil one. Memorize Hebrews 4:12 as a weapon against the enemy and his attacks.

> For the word of God is living and active, sharper than any two-edged sword, piercing to the division of soul and of spirit, of joints and of marrow, and discerning the thoughts and intentions of the heart.
>
> —HEBREWS 4:12

# DAY 2

# SATAN'S SECOND ATTACK

READ GENESIS 3:4-7.

*But the serpent said to the woman, "You will not surely die. For God knows that when you eat of it your eyes will be opened, and you will be like God, knowing good and evil." So when the woman saw that the tree was good for food, and that it was a delight to the eyes, and that the tree was to be desired to make one wise, she took of its fruit and ate, and she also gave some to her husband who was with her, and he ate. Then the eyes of both were opened, and they knew that they were naked. And they sewed fig leaves together and made themselves loincloths.*

After tempting Eve with his first attack—doubting God's Word—Satan perfectly set her up for his second attack. In Genesis 3:4-5, the serpent tempted her to doubt God's goodness. He was able to convince her that God was holding something back from her. God's goodness to Adam and Eve couldn't have been more real—He was keeping them from knowing evil.

Satan said Eve would not die if she ate the fruit; however, he did not say eating this fruit would separate her from the Source of life. Although her physical life would continue, her innocence died that day in the garden, and each day after would bring her closer to physical death—something God did not intend for humanity to experience.

When have you experienced unintended consequences for your sin?

Eve fell into Satan's trap, and Adam fell right along with her (see Gen. 3:6). He failed to speak God's Word and refute the lies of Satan. This led Adam and Eve to fall into sin. Their fall resulted in the entire human race falling into sin equally (see Rom. 5:12). To better understand how Satan attacks you, look at the following table and see how the three of Eve's statements connect with three categories of sin we all are tempted to fall into every day.

|  | LUST OF THE FLESH | LUST OF THE EYES | PRIDE OF LIFE |
|---|---|---|---|
| **Genesis 3:5-6** | "the woman saw that the tree was good for food" | "and that it was a delight to the eyes," | "and that the tree was to be desired to make one wise" |
| **What it Means** | Eve knew the food would satisfy her physical appetite | Eve saw the food looked delicious, and she desired more while looking at it | Eve wanted what God had and decided to take it for herself |

James 1:14-15 says, "But each person is tempted when he is lured and enticed by his desire. Then desire when it has conceived gives birth to sin, and sin when it is fully grown brings forth death." We are tempted every day in the same way Adam and Eve were. We might not be tempted by the fruit of a tree, but there are probably things in our lives that we continually struggle with that do not please God.

Which of the three types of sin listed in the chart do you struggle with the most? What is one way you can more faithfully turn to God when you feel tempted?

"But each person is tempted when he is lured and enticed by his desire. Then desire when it has conceived gives birth to sin, and sin when it is fully grown brings forth death."

—JAMES 1:14-15

Take some time today and read Psalm 25:7 and 2 Corinthians 5:21. Consider the types of sin you have struggled with overcoming since you were younger. Then, think about the things in life right now that tempt you to doubt God's Word and His goodness toward you.

Close today in prayer. Ask God to remind you of His goodness and to help you never doubt His eternal love. Identify your areas of struggle and ask God to help you find accountability, relief from temptation, and a desire to flee from the sins that seem to tangle you up most often.

# DAY 3

# OUR EXAMPLE TO RESIST TEMPTATION

Since we all know each of us has not lived a life without sin, we can admit we have fallen into the temptations of the lust of the flesh, the lust of the eyes, and the pride of life. Admitting this helps us realize we do not have the power to defeat sin or death. We need someone to help us gain victory in this life. The good news is that someone is Jesus!

Take time to read Matthew 4:1-11 and then look at the table below to see how Jesus responded to the same attacks Satan used to deceive Eve.

READ MATTHEW 4:1-11.

|  | LUST OF THE FLESH | LUST OF THE EYES | PRIDE OF LIFE |
|---|---|---|---|
| **Satan's Words** | "If you are the Son of God, command these stones to become loaves of bread." | "If you are the Son of God, throw yourself down, for it is written, 'He will command his angels concerning you,' and 'On their hands they will bear you up, lest you strike your foot against a stone.'" | "All these I will give you, if you will fall down and worship me." |
| **Jesus's Use of God's Word** | "It is written, 'Man shall not live by bread alone, but by every word that comes from the mouth of God.'" | "Again it is written, 'You shall not put the Lord your God to the test.'" | "Be gone, Satan! For it is written,' You shall worship the Lord your God and him only shall you serve.'" |

| What It Means | Satan knew Jesus hadn't eaten in forty days, so he tempted Jesus to use His powers as God to meet His physical needs. Yet, Jesus responded using the same weapon we have today—God's Word. | Satan took Jesus to the top of the temple in Jerusalem and tried to use Scripture to tempt Jesus. Jesus knew Scripture's whole and true meaning, and He responded by quoting God's Word to overcome Satan. | Satan promised Jesus could rule the world's kingdoms if Jesus would worship him. Jesus knew Satan didn't have the power to make this promise, and He loved the Father above all. So, He remained faithful, quoted Scripture, and was victorious over Satan. |
| --- | --- | --- | --- |

When we run to Jesus and embrace Him as Lord, not only are our sins forgiven (see Eph. 1:7), but also the perfect life of Jesus now covers us. Jesus understands our struggles and wants us to run to Him to fight against temptation.

Read Hebrews 4:14-16. How does knowing Jesus understands everything we experience as humans but remained sinless as a human help you fight temptation and sin?

Today, read Ephesians 6:17 and think about how taking up the sword of the Spirit means to quote Scripture when Satan tempts us. Scripture was a valuable weapon that Jesus used to fight temptation. He has given us this same weapon, but it's up to us to use it and walk in the victory He has already won for us and given to us.

Close today in prayer. Ask God to give you a hunger for His Word so that you can deploy it as a weapon against Satan in times of temptation.

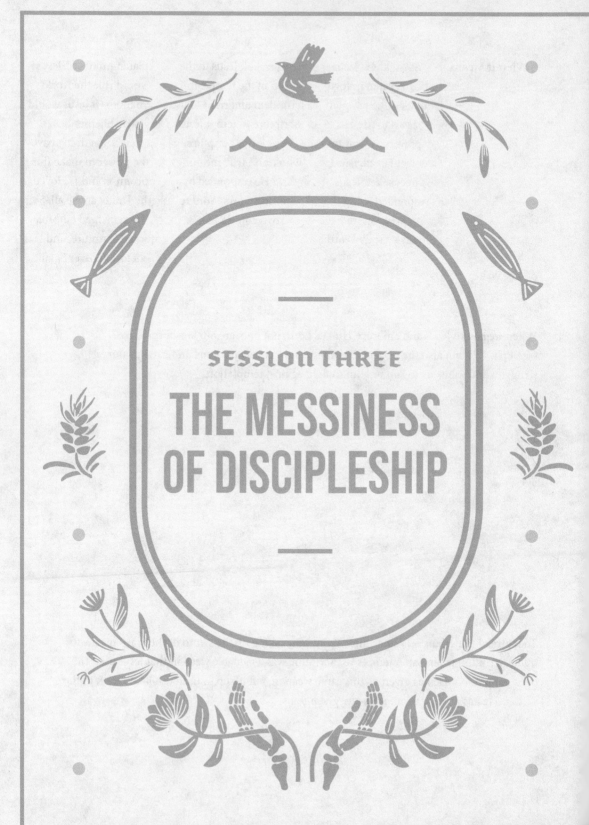

SESSION THREE

# THE MESSINESS OF DISCIPLESHIP

**EPHESIANS 4:25-32**

Therefore, having put away falsehood, let each one of you speak the truth with his neighbor, for we are members one of another. Be angry and do not sin; do not let the sun go down on your anger, and give no opportunity to the devil. Let the thief no longer steal, but rather let him labor, doing honest work with his own hands, so that he may have something to share with anyone in need. Let no corrupting talk come out of your mouths, but only such as is good for building up, as fits the occasion, that it may give grace to those who hear. And do not grieve the Holy Spirit of God, by whom you were sealed for the day of redemption. Let all bitterness and wrath and anger and clamor and slander be put away from you, along with all malice. Be kind to one another, tenderhearted, forgiving one another, as God in Christ forgave you.

# VIDEO

> "Let no corrupting talk come out of your mouths, but only such as is good for building up, as fits the occasion, that it may give grace to those who hear."
>
> — EPHESIANS 4:29

Don't worry about it. The bill has been taken care of. The debt is _____.

Holistic discipleship corrects our _____, calls out our _____, and combats our _____.

Discipleship is messy, because it begins to deal with all of the things in our hearts that are _____ to God.

God also calls out our _____.

# GROUP DISCUSSION

FOCUS STATEMENT:

**Holistic Discipleship corrects our speech, calls out our selfishness, and combats our sinfulness.**

Juneteenth, short for "June Nineteenth," marks the day when federal troops arrived in Galveston, Texas, in 1865 to ensure that all enslaved people were set free. This was necessary because some slave-owners refused to release the people they had enslaved. On top of that, the people who had been enslaved had to learn how to be free. It's not easy to change patterns of behavior and thought when you've only known one way of living.

What are some challenges to retraining your mind and behavior when you experience major changes in life?

Our journey as followers of Jesus is similar. Since we have been set free from the power and slavery of sin through Christ, the evil one, the world, and even our internal desires, don't want us to realize we are free. Discipleship helps us know how to walk in the freedom Jesus has given us from slavery to sin. It can be a messy process, but it's worth it!

## DISCIPLESHIP CORRECTS OUR SPEECH

READ EPHESIANS 4:25-27.

Speaking the truth and putting away lying is vital to correcting our speech. There are at least three different ways we lie: We lie when we purposefully add details to the facts; we lie when we withhold truthful information from others, only giving them the portion of the truth we want them to hear; and we lie when we make commitments and promises we don't intend to keep.

Which of these three forms of lying do you struggle with the most? Why?

No one has to teach us to lie; we do it naturally, like it's our native language. This is a result of our fall into sin (see Gen. 3). Discipleship confronts lying because it comes with accountability. When we enter a discipleship relationship, we invite those walking with us to have insight into the things that can fuel our desire to lie—our hearts, minds, and past experiences.

Discipleship not only helps us tell the truth, but it also assists us in watching the tone we use with others when we talk. Proverbs 15:1 says, "A soft answer turns away wrath, but a harsh word stirs up anger." Our tone can easily distract people from the truth we want to share. Discipleship addresses the tone we use no matter the circumstances we face.

When has someone's tone of voice turned you away from the truth he or she wanted to share with you?

Discipleship is the remedy for lying and speaking with harsh tones because it centers on God's Word, which is full of truth. The more truth we speak, the less opportunity we create for telling lies. Discipleship gives us relationships in which we can be known and deeply loved, so love and truth become present in our actions and words.

When God wants to address our speech, He's not just concerned with the words we say and how we say them—He's concerned with the emotions behind them too. He wants to address what's in our hearts. In Ephesians 4:26-27, Paul said, "Be angry and do not sin; do not let the sun go down on your anger, and give no opportunity to the devil." Notice he didn't say being angry is always a sin. Anger is an emotion God has given us. We must remember there are two types of anger:

- **Righteous Anger** – This kind of anger is over actions done by others that are harmful, but our response is to work to right the wrong. For example, Jesus overturning the tables in the temple in Matthew 21:12-17.

- **Unrighteous Anger** – This kind of anger focuses on how to make others pay for what they've done, pushing God out of the way so we can take matters into our own hands. Cain's murder of his brother Able in Genesis 4:1-16 is an example of where unrighteous anger can lead.

We must remember—we're not Jesus. Righteous anger can become unrighteous quickly, if allowed to linger in our hearts. That's why Paul said, "Give no opportunity to the devil" (Eph. 4:27). Discipleship deals with everything in our hearts, speech, and relationships, so everyone in the body of Christ can grow healthy together—even if it's messy!

## DISCIPLESHIP CALLS OUT OUR SELFISHNESS

READ EPHESIANS 4:28-29.

On the surface, Ephesians 4:28 may not clearly connect to selfishness, but it's there. Selfishness is what fuels stealing. Stealing is not a lifestyle God wants for His children. Our discipleship relationships help flip the selfishness of stealing into the generosity of sharing with those in need.

Stealing is something I've struggled with, and my temptation to steal did not go away immediately after Jesus saved me. One day a few years after I became a follower of Jesus, I received a call from my mother. I could tell in her voice something wasn't right. I knew why she was calling. A few weeks earlier, I went to my mom and dad's house and took the debit card out of my dad's wallet while he slept. I went to a nearby ATM and withdrew some money. As a result, my mom and dad did not have enough money in their account to pay their bills.

My mom plainly asked me, "Damon, did you take any money from our bank account without asking us?" I knew I had to stop this pattern of stealing by not covering it up with a lie. I took a deep breath before saying, "Yes, I did." My mom thanked me for being honest and not lying. She also shared how hurt she was because of my actions. I confessed that I didn't want to steal anymore. My mom then said, "Damon, if you truly want to walk in repentance for stealing, you need to open up this area of your life to your wife and men from our church."

God used my mom to call me into a discipleship relationship where people in my life could walk with me and help me grow to be more Christlike. I took my mom's advice, and while painful and embarrassing at the start, the result was a greater level of character development in my walk with Jesus. To God's glory, I never stole from my mom and dad again.

At what point in D.A.'s story was he selfish? Where was he unselfish? How could things have been different if he had chosen to continue to be selfish?

Inside our discipleship relationships, we should be working together to develop life rhythms showing we're responsible with all the resources God has trusted us with. This goes back to Genesis 1:28. God gave humanity the privilege and responsibility of being "caretakers" of all the world, including all things living.[3] God has entrusted us to create culture. We create culture when we engage with other humans and the world God placed us in. The culture we make can be helpful or harmful to us, others, and even the planet.

Creating helpful culture provides us with opportunities to serve others by meeting their needs. In doing this, we do not allow selfishness to drive our decisions. The result is seeing generosity become normal. The early church modeled this for us. In Acts 2:45, we read how the early church pooled its resources to meet the needs of others.

When have you been blessed by someone else's generosity?

In Ephesians 4:29 Paul explained that our speech should not only encourage the person we are speaking to but anyone who is nearby and hears that our words are full of truth, tender in tone, and timely. When they hear such words, they too receive comfort and encouragement. Discipleship that helps us remove our selfishness is crucial because it has the potential to help so many other people.

Words without selfishness are:

TRUTHFUL  >  TENDER IN TONE  >  TIMELY

# DISCIPLESHIP COMBATS OUR SINFULNESS

## READ EPHESIANS 4:30-32.

Ephesians 4:30 gives us insight into why we must combat sinfulness. The word "grieve" implies deep emotional and mental distress. The actions of our old way of life, prior to knowing Jesus, grieve the Holy Spirit, who dwells in every believer. The "old self" also causes grief to those we're living in discipleship with. This is why discipleship is messy!

We must walk in sensitivity to the Holy Spirit in order to obey His leading. The beauty of the Holy Spirit is that He remains with us even when we cause Him grief.

How do you walk in sensitivity to the Holy Spirit?

A healthy relationship with the Holy Spirit will overflow into every other relationship we have. When we don't hold on to resentment toward others, we remove the opportunity for bitterness to enter our hearts. When we use the Holy Spirit's strength, we become patient even under pressure. When we forgive others as Christ has forgiven us, we leave no room for unrighteous anger to linger. When we have a tender tone when speaking the truth to those who have hurt us, we fight against clamor (emotional outbursts) and slander (abusive language). Eliminating sins like this removes the desire to seek revenge.

As we align with the Holy Spirit's leading, we'll become prone to be kind to one another and tenderhearted by showing others our concern. You will be better equipped to serve the church if you engage and remain in holistic discipleship relationships now rather than waiting to start when you are older. Hang in there, even if it's messy!

As you close this time of discussion with your group, pray for one another to remain faithful to the process of discipleship, even if it gets messy. Remember that the Holy Spirit is with you always and desires to equip, guide, and counsel you as you grow in your relationship with Him.

# DAY 1

# CONFESSION

READ PSALM 51.

Before the first verse of Psalm 51, notice the phrase "to the choirmaster" in the heading. This means Psalm 51 was written and delivered to the Chief Musician for public reciting and singing. Think about that for a moment. David's confession of sin was not written for private meditation and personal reflection only—everyone in the kingdom would know. As the king, not only was he the most visible figure in Israel, but he also needed to model for his people what it looked like to confess sin, seek God's forgiveness, and walk in repentance after. We can learn from this example too.

What do you feel inside when you think about everyone knowing your deepest, darkest secret or worst mistake?

David's sin was clearly identified. The title of the Psalm reads, "A Psalm of David when Nathan the Prophet Went to Him After He Had Gone in to Bathsheba." You see, David had a very human moment, and he did not come clean until he was caught. But God loved David so much that He sent the prophet Nathan to confront him about his sins of adultery and murder (see 2 Sam. 12:1-15). This gave the king an opportunity to repent and confess.

When have you been confronted about your sin? How did you respond?

When we embrace Jesus, God forgives all of our sins because of Jesus's shed blood (see Eph. 1:7). We will never face God's eternal wrath for our sins because Jesus took all of it in our place while on the cross. Isaiah 53:5-6 paints a vivid picture of our sin debt being laid on Jesus. The punishment for our sin fell on Jesus so that we might be free. Now we stand before God, not condemned, but free from the eternal power of sin (see Rom. 8:1).

Does knowing that you stand before God and are not condemned because of what Jesus did for you help you have courage to confess your sin to Him? Why or why not?

It's important to remember that all of our sins—past and future—are forgiven in Christ, but the consequences of our choices remain. This was evident in David's life as well. When we fall into sin, we must run to Him instead of away from Him. When we face the consequences of our sins, we can know we're still forgiven while we deal with the results of our choices. God is for us, and He loves us. He demonstrated His love for us while we were still dead in our sins and running away from Him (see Rom. 5:6-8). Don't let any past or present sins keep you from being close to God the Father. Run to Him and be with Him; He desires your company today.

Close today in prayer. Examine your heart and see if you have any unconfessed sin. Confess any sin the Holy Spirit brings to mind and consider if this is something you need to confess to another believer you are in a discipleship relationship with.

# DAY 2

# CONFRONTATION

READ PSALM 51:1-2.

*Have mercy on me, O God, according to your steadfast love; according to your abundant mercy blot out my transgressions. Wash me thoroughly from my iniquity, and cleanse me from my sin!*

David realized his sin made him guilty. He knew what he did and tried to cover it up. David's guilt greatly effected his relationship with God. So, David pleaded for God to have compassion on him. When he begged God to have mercy on him, David used the impersonal Hebrew word "God" instead of the covenant-keeping name of God (YHWH) he typically used before. Perhaps this was because his guilt forced him to reckon with the fact that he was a covenant breaker, and he feared God no longer wanted to honor His covenant with David. David felt the distance he created between himself and God.

When has a decision you made put distance between you and God?

I sympathize with David, and maybe you do too. The distance I feel from God when I sin causes me to feel unworthy of even mentioning his name. But David didn't stay there, and neither should we. David asked God to have mercy on him "according to" God's "steadfast love." God always keeps His promises, and David pleaded with Him to extend His never-failing, covenant-keeping love to a covenant breaker like him! David knew he could not earn this love and didn't deserve it. David knew his heart was bankrupt, and he desperately needed God to fill him with peace and joy once again.

How do you see God? Do you see Him as a loving, covenant-keeping Father like David or something else? Explain.

One of the best ways we can express the constant love we receive from God is by sharing His faithful love with others who have fallen into sin. Many times we feel comfortable in the darkness of hidden sin, which keeps us trapped. Refusing to confess sin is like putting ourselves in a prison cell with no door. We can leave anytime but choose to keep ourselves trapped because of our refusal to confess our sin. What we often fail to realize is that true freedom lies on the other side of confession.

What are some ways you can help others who refuse to confess their sins to God?

Because God loves people faithfully and knows what is best, if they remain stubborn and refuse to confess, He may shine a light on their situation and make it known so those they're in discipleship relationships with can help them walk out of the darkness. This is why Galatians 6:1 says, "Brothers if anyone is caught in any transgression, you who are spiritual should restore him in a spirit of gentleness. Keep watch on yourself, lest you too be tempted." The ministry of mercy God wants us to share with those trapped in sin includes tenderly sharing the truth of God's Word when they're brought out of the darkness and into the light. We should not beat them up and kick them while they're down. Instead, we should breathe grace and truth on them so God can restore them inside a safe culture of grace.

Take some time today to reflect on how much God loves you and how He will never cancel you because you struggle with sin. He shows you grace so you can do the same with others. Creating grace culture rises and falls on our ability to know that God will not cancel us, so we should not seek to cancel others.

# DAY 3

# COMPASSION

READ PSALM 51:3-5.

*For I know my transgressions, and my sin is ever before me. Against you, you only, have I sinned and done what is evil in your sight, so that you may be justified in your words and blameless in your judgment. Behold, I was brought forth in iniquity, and in sin did my mother conceive me.*

Grace culture calls us to take ownership of our sins against God by not passing the blame on others. This is exactly what David did in verses 3 and 4. Think about it this way: throughout Bathsheba's pregnancy, David wrestled with the tension of unconfessed sin, which led to his hard heart. Remember his response to Nathan's illustration of the lamb. (If you need a refresher, read 2 Samuel 12:1-15.) David was cold, unforgiving, and ruthless. He was ready to cancel the villain in the story until he was told that he was that villain!

This should lead us to ask ourselves: When I have unconfessed sin, do I see the sins of others the same way David saw the villain's in Nathan's story? If anyone is a candidate for modeling compassion, it should be Christians because we've received compassion from God, but hardened hearts cause us to withhold it from each other and the world.

When you hear of someone else's sin being exposed, how do you normally respond toward them in your heart?

David traced his sin nature back to conception by saying, "behold I was brought forth in iniquity, and in sin did my mother conceive me" (v. 5). David was saying, "From my conception, sin has been woven into the fabric of my makeup, and I alone am responsible for my sinfulness." This truth should keep us compassionate toward others; we were born in the same condition they are still in. Integrity leads us to admit we're wrong, which is counter-cultural in our day. People want to blame everyone else to keep from acknowledging their own sins.

Is it hard for you to admit when you've sinned? Why or why not?

To operate in compassion, we must follow the example of David, who opened his whole heart to God. God wants our complete honesty, and those far from Him deserve to see us live in transparency. As we walk in this humility and are restored to a place of spiritual health (see Gal. 6:1-2), we can consider how to teach others about the rich mercies and abundant grace of God.

How would you describe the rich mercies and abundant grace of God to someone who is struggling with sin?

David knew God's mercies and said, "then I will teach transgressors your ways, and sinners will return to you" (Ps. 51:13). Since David had been forgiven, he was a qualified candidate to show those living with unconfessed sin who they could go to for forgiveness. This is one of our roles in sharing the gospel with as many people as possible and not canceling anyone, desiring to show everyone grace. No matter where God sends you, cling to the cross and steward the gospel well by living in transparency. If you are clinging to unconfessed sin, come clean under the loving grace of our God. Your home, community, school, city, and our whole world desperately need Christians who will lead with integrity by confessing their sins to God and confronting their shame with the gospel to model compassion to those far from Him. So let's be the ones they've been looking for!

Ask God to help you with your compassion. If you need to be reminded of the great sin debt Jesus paid for you on the cross, take some time to focus on that. Then, ask Him to help you show that great compassion to others who need to be delivered from their bondage to sin.

SESSION FOUR

# CREATING GRACE CULTURE

COLOSSIANS 3:12-15

Put on then, as God's chosen ones, holy and beloved, compassionate hearts, kindness, humility, meekness, and patience, bearing with one another and, if one has a complaint against another, forgiving each other; as the Lord has forgiven you, so you also must forgive. And above all these put on love, which binds everything together in perfect harmony. And let the peace of Christ rule in your hearts, to which indeed you were called in one body. And be thankful.

# VIDEO

> Put on then, as God's chosen ones, holy and beloved, compassionate hearts, kindness, humility, meekness, and patience, bearing with one another and, if one has a complaint against another, forgiving each other; as the Lord has forgiven you, so you also must forgive.
>
> — COLOSSIANS 3:12-13

Cancel culture focuses on _____ an individual.

Grace culture: gives _____, _____, and _____ because we're all in a journey, seeking to grow in Christ.

Holy means to be set _____ from everything and everyone else.

When you embrace Jesus, you are clothed in Jesus's _____.

Creating grace culture is the best environment for us to grow in our relationship with _____ and with _____ _____.

Grace comes with _____.

Grace culture says, "Let's walk in the _____ Jesus has given us."

# GROUP DISCUSSION

FOCUS STATEMENT:

Grace is a gift Christians have received that is thoroughly enjoyed when shared with others.

We live in a time when people get canceled faster than the blink of an eye. People are canceled, not just for abusive and harmful behaviors, but for doing or saying anything that is perceived to be against what is acceptable in the dominant culture. This even happens within the church.

The best way to change cancel culture is to create a culture that is in direct contrast to it. We must consider how we, as followers of Jesus, can create a culture of grace. Look at how cancel culture and grace culture differ.

|  | CANCEL CULTURE | GRACE CULTURE |
|---|---|---|
| FAILURE | Focuses on shaming people for their failures | Embraces the gospel so that Jesus's righteousness covers shame (see 2 Cor. 5:21) |
| JUSTICE | Seeks retaliation and revenge | Points to the cross, where Jesus took the punishment for our sin (see 1 Pet. 2:21-25) |
| RELATIONSHIPS | Aims to break down, dissolve, and destroy relationships | Aims to reconcile and restore relationships (see Col. 3:13) |
| PERSONAL GROWTH | Keeps bringing up past failures | Affirms maturity through discipleship (see Eph. 4:11-16) |

It's important to understand grace is not one-directional (only from God to us). Having a one-directional view of grace cheapens it and allows us to be spiritually lazy. The grace given to us flows from God to us and then from us to those in our home, neighborhood, school, work, church, those we engage online, and everywhere else. Grace is a gift God has given to us. Like all gifts, it is free to receive, but we must steward it well.

How have you seen cancel culture affect others?

## WE'RE ALL TROPHIES OF GRACE

READ COLOSSIANS 3:12.

The first step in creating grace culture is for each of us who follow Jesus to realize we are His trophies of grace. In Colossians 3:12, Paul refers to believers as, "God's chosen ones, holy and beloved." To be God's "chosen ones" means God loves us with a never-ending love, despite our past. We were born in sin and still commit sin, but God made us holy through Jesus. The word "holy" means to be separate from things that are basic or regular.

Which one of these three descriptors in Colossians 3:12 do you struggle the most to believe—that you are chosen, holy, or beloved? Why?

A great way to think about the separate nature of holiness is a trophy case. Think about how a school's trophies won through academic, band, and athletic competitions are set apart from lockers, books, cafeteria trays, and everyday school supplies. The trophies have been placed inside a protected showcase, handled with care, and seen as unique. Each trophy has its own story as to how it was earned. As believers, we have been set apart like trophies as a showcase for the glory, love, and goodness of Jesus.

The word "beloved" also means God loves every single follower of Jesus equally. He doesn't show favoritism. As trophies of grace, we must all remember Romans 5:6, "For while we were still weak, at the right time, Christ died for the ungodly." Not one trophy of grace has an edge over any other. Jesus died for all of us—each while we were still lost in our sin. Ultimately, this reveals His equal love for every person.

## RESPECT ALL OTHER TROPHIES OF GRACE

Step two in creating grace culture is found in the second part of Colossians 3:12. We learn to respect all other trophies of grace by having compassionate hearts and showing kindness, humility, meekness, and patience. We are more likely to show respect to others when we apply these characteristics Paul commands us to put on.

Let's look at each of these words more closely to see how they help us respect each other as trophies of grace. **Compassion** describes a genuine, tender sensitivity toward others. **Kindness** is demonstrated when we act on compassion toward others. **Humility** is having a realistic view of ourselves. God has blessed each of us with different abilities, gifts, and talents; and the Holy Spirit has provided every follower of Jesus with spiritual gifts to build up other followers of Jesus. Humility helps us recognize the abilities and spiritual gifts God has given us so we can serve others in the areas where we are gifted or strong while allowing others to help us in our areas of weakness. This shows respect in real time.

Which comes more naturally to you—compassion, kindness, or humility? Why? Which is more of a struggle for you? Why?

Showing **meekness**, or gentleness, is when we consider how our actions affect others. Gentleness can be demonstrated when we use social media to encourage others rather than trolling or tearing down. **Patience** means to operate with self-control even when circumstances are frustrating. Since we are God's trophies of grace, our actions should reflect Jesus's victory in our lives over pride and selfishness. We reveal this by having compassionate hearts, kindness, humility, meekness, and patience.

How can practicing gentleness, which can lead to self-control, reveal respect to other trophies of grace?

# GRACE COMES WITH HEALTHY BOUNDARIES

Since life throws us all types of challenges, we must consider how to keep showing respect to others while not allowing people to take advantage of us and hurt us. Our third and final step helps us frame boundaries to protect our hearts.

READ COLOSSIANS 3:13-15.

We know that during this life, we will not always walk in perfect obedience to Jesus; other followers of Jesus won't either. The gospel is the only message that says—no matter the differences we may have in the areas of preferences, hobbies, sports teams, or even past mistakes and trauma—we are all equally loved by God. These truths are essential in understanding what it means to bear with someone. To "bear with" someone means to patiently endure those whose actions and opinions you may disagree with.

How can you respectfully disagree with someone you have to "bear with"?

Developing healthy boundaries comes by having hard conversations that lead to a mutual understanding of how to move forward. There will be times when we hurt others or are hurt by others. Jesus knew this would be a reality, and Scripture clarifies how we can work through such offenses. The Bible tells us to forgive as we have been forgiven (see Col. 3:13). Forgiveness does not mean we remain silent or fail to seek justice when we've been hurt. When we've been hurt or abused, we must share our stories with the proper authorities to help bring justice and prevent others from being hurt or abused. However, we do not take matters into our own hands and seek to get back at those who hurt us.

As Paul said in Colossians 3:14, we are called to operate in love. As we work to create grace culture, love means we work to have reconciliation in our broken relationships. These next two scenarios help us know how to seek out reconciliation with others:

1.  **When we sin against others:** We should confess our sin to them, and ask for forgiveness. If they forgive us, we have reconciliation. If they do not, we can rest in the knowledge that we did what God calls us to do when we wrong someone else (see Matt. 5:23-24). Among Christians, our goal should be to strive for reconciliation when we sin against each other.

2.  **When others sin against us:** Seek out the one who has offended you and in gentleness and self-control, explain what they did and how they hurt you. If they repent and apologize, we have reconciliation (see Matt. 18:15). If someone seeks you out and asks for forgiveness, forgive them (see Luke 17:4). However, there may be times when those who hurt us refuse to acknowledge their wrong. Showing love to them may mean letting the relationship with them go and allowing God to help them grow and heal as you forgive and heal. Forgiveness is a process, but as Jesus—our example in all things—offered forgiveness with some of His last breaths (see Luke 23:34), we can learn how to forgive too.

When have you experienced either of these two scenarios in your life? How did things work out for you?

When we respond by following Scripture and under the influence of the Holy Spirit, we will act in love. Love binds us together, and when we seek reconciliation, we let the peace of Christ rule in our hearts. The word "peace" means joining something broken, divided, or separated. This type of peace heals brokenness, division, and separation. Only the love of God can promise and deliver something this grand.

Cancel culture breaks, divides, and separates relationships, but grace culture works to bring healing and restoration. A culture of grace is present when the peace of Christ rules in people's hearts (see Col. 3:15). A culture of grace inside the frame of healthy boundaries gives us the freedom to live in peaceful relationships we're thankful for. We then advertise our peace and thankfulness by using grace to season everything about our lives.

As you close this time of discussion with your group, pray that you would see each other as trophies of God's grace. Ask God to help you learn to respect each other and set up healthy boundaries to protect your hearts.

# DAY 1

# JOSEPH AND FORGIVENESS

READ GENESIS 37; 39-50.

The life of Joseph gives us an honest, up close, and personal view at what forgiving those who have sinned against us looks like. In Genesis 37, Joseph's brothers hated how much their father favored him, so they conspired to kill him. Then under the leadership of their brother Judah, they sold him into slavery. In Genesis 39, Joseph excelled in his role and was put in charge of Potiphar's house. Potiphar's wife tried to seduce Joseph, but he refused, knowing that would dishonor both God and Potiphar. Angry at his rejection, Potiphar's wife lied and said Joseph tried to assault her sexually. Joseph was thrown in prison and remained there.

Have you ever been wrongly accused? What happened? What has God taught you from the experience?

The Bible tells us God remained with Joseph the entire time. God gave Joseph the ability to interpret dreams, and while in prison, he was able to correctly interpret the dreams of two fellow prisoners who had been in service to Pharoah. One of the prisoners was executed, but the other returned to Pharoah's service. However, when the cupbearer was restored, he did not tell Pharoah about Joseph (see Gen. 40:23). Then Pharoah had troubling dreams, and the former prisoner remembered Joseph and his ability to interpret dreams. Joseph was brought before Pharoah and correctly interpreted the dreams. So Joseph was removed from prison and became a high official in the Egyptian government (see Gen. 41). During this time, a famine came over the land. Due to Joseph's interpretation of Pharaoh's dreams, Egypt was prepared for it. This famine was so widespread that Joseph's brothers had to travel to Egypt, where there was enough grain, to ask for food so their family could survive.

When has God turned a terrible circumstance in your life into something good? What happened?

Instead of killing his brothers, who sold him into slavery, Joseph forgave them. He provided space for his whole family to move to Egypt and live and flourish with him. Joseph said something powerful in Genesis 50:20, "As for you, you meant evil against me, but God meant it for good, to bring it about that many people should be kept alive as they are today." In our lives, the ones who hurt us may have had evil intentions; however, now that we are in Christ, no matter what evil they did to us, God desires to use it for His glory and the good of us and others.

Take some time today to consider how the wounds you have received from others can be given to God for Him to heal and use for your good, the good of others, and His glory.

# DAY 2

# PRAYER AND FORGIVENESS

Reading about the life of Joseph used to make me feel inadequate. How could I ever forgive the way he forgave his brothers? Maybe you've felt the same way. For the next two days, I want to walk through a passage of Scripture that helped me understand how prayer is central to forgiveness and, through the example and teaching of Jesus, how I learned to forgive.

> READ LUKE 11:9-10.

*And I tell you, ask, and it will be given to you; seek, and you will find; knock, and it will be opened to you. For everyone who asks receives, and the one who seeks finds, and to the one who knocks it will be opened.*

This passage follows Jesus teaching His disciples the model prayer (see Luke 11:1-4). Jesus expects us to pray to God the Father regularly. Let's break down the model prayer and look more closely to see exactly what Jesus was explaining to His disciples.

- When we pray, we should refer to God as our Father and praise Him for the great things He has done in our lives, everyone else's lives, and throughout all creation (see Luke 11:2).

- We are to ask for His rule (kingdom) to be made visible through our lives on earth, just like it is in heaven (see Luke 11:2).

- We are to share with Him our needs like children do with their parents or guardians (see Luke 11:3).

- We are also to ask for God's forgiveness as we seek to forgive those who have sinned against us (see Luke 11:4).

- Finally, we must ask God to help us avoid and fight off temptation (see Luke 11:4).

Which portion of the Model Prayer do you find easiest to pray? Why? Which portion is the hardest for you to pray? Why?

Jesus tells us to keep asking, seeking, and knocking. He means for us to ask, seek, and knock through our prayer life. God gives us perfectly timed gifts, and Jesus guarantees us the Father will answer our prayers. Sometimes He will say yes. Other times, He will say no. Sometimes He will tell us to keep praying about it. Just because we don't get the answer we want doesn't mean God is not answering.

Jesus promises that the Father hears our prayers and will respond according to His will. This doesn't mean we have a green light to get whatever we want; it means that when we seek after Him, He aligns our hearts to His desires. When we have His desires primary in our hearts and when we ask for something He desires, He will give it to us. This includes the desire and ability to forgive those who have hurt us.

How has God shaped your desires to line up more with His over time through prayer?

Forgiveness is hard. Jesus knows that. That's why He included it in His model prayer. All believers, for all time, should long to forgive those who have wronged them. Why? Because Jesus forgave us for all the ways we've wronged Him. Grace culture comes when, through the power of the Holy Spirit in us, we learn to forgive as we've been forgiven.

Take some time today to examine if there is any unforgiveness in your heart. If there is, pray that God would help turn your heart to His desire to forgive as He has forgiven you.

DAY 3

# FATHERS AND FORGIVENESS

READ LUKE 11:11-13.

*What father among you, if his son asks for a fish, will instead of a fish give him a serpent; or if he asks for an egg, will give him a scorpion? If you then, who are evil, know how to give good gifts to your children, how much more will the heavenly Father give the Holy Spirit to those who ask him!"*

In Luke 11:11-13, Jesus wants us to understand how good God the Father is toward us so that we will not be scared to share with Him the needs we have in life. As a father myself, I can relate to this. When my children ask me for food or snacks, I don't give them poison or something they cannot eat, like a rock. I'm not perfect, but because I love my children, I will do all I can to provide for them. For some, the word *father* is a challenge. Some people don't know their biological dad, or suffered abuse from him, or have been hurt by him before. Not all people have a good relationship with their earthly father.

How would you describe your relationship with your earthly father?

What we can't do is charge the sins of our earthly fathers to God the Father as if He's the One who hurt us. In the verses we read today, Jesus shared what He did about God the Father's character because He wants us to know that even if we don't trust our earthly dads, we can always trust our heavenly Father.

How would you describe your relationship with your heavenly Father?

This is the point Jesus was making: If our imperfect fathers, mothers, family members, and friends can give us things that benefit us, how much more should we trust God the Father, who is perfect, to provide us with the good gifts we need? He desires for us to represent both His holiness and His kingdom well. He does this by giving us good gifts and helping us as we seek to live for Him.

How have you experienced the goodness of God the Father in your life?

We can live for God by surrendering to the Holy Spirit, who lives inside of every believer (see Rom. 8:9-13). God doesn't just want to give us forgiveness alone. He desires to provide us with all we need to have an enjoyable relationship with Him and others. This includes our earthly fathers and anyone who may have hurt us in the past. We can achieve peace in our hearts from past hurts through Jesus and learning, through His power in us, to forgive.

Trust God today by asking for the resources you need to follow Him closely daily. That might mean forgiving your earthly father or someone else who has hurt you.

SESSION FIVE

# ABIDING IN JESUS

## JOHN 15:1-11

"I am the true vine, and my Father is the vinedresser. Every branch in me that does not bear fruit he takes away, and every branch that does bear fruit he prunes, that it may bear more fruit. Already you are clean because of the word that I have spoken to you. Abide in me, and I in you. As the branch cannot bear fruit by itself, unless it abides in the vine, neither can you, unless you abide in me. I am the vine; you are the branches. Whoever abides in me and I in him, he it is that bears much fruit, for apart from me you can do nothing. If anyone does not abide in me he is thrown away like a branch and withers; and the branches are gathered, thrown into the fire, and burned. If you abide in me, and my words abide in you, ask whatever you wish, and it will be done for you. By this my Father is glorified, that you bear much fruit and so prove to be my disciples. As the Father has loved me, so have I loved you. Abide in my love. If you keep my commandments, you will abide in my love, just as I have kept my Father's commandments and abide in his love. These things I have spoken to you, that my joy may be in you, and that your joy may be full."

# VIDEO

> "I am the vine; you are the branches. Whoever abides in Me and I in him, he it is that bears much fruit, for apart from Me you an do nothing."
>
> — JOHN 15:5

Abiding in Jesus in tough times will give us the
_____ to understand the depth
of the meaningfulness of our relationship with God.

How do we abide in Jesus during _____-
_____?

"I am the true vine, and my Father is the vinedresser.
Every branch in me that does not bear fruit he takes
away, and every branch that does bear fruit he prunes,
that it may bear more fruit." —John 15:1-2

Jesus is the _____.

God created us to walk in obedience to His commands
that would lead to a life of _____ even
when the hard times hit us.

Being connected to Christ is like being connected to a
_____ _____.

"Already you are clean because of the word that I have spoken to you. Abide in me, and I in you.
As the branch cannot bear fruit by itself, unless it abides in the vine, neither can you, unless you
abide in me." —John 15:3-4

_____ still remain even when _____ has been given.

Being in Christ gives us the _____ to bear fruit.

God is cleansing you. He loves you. He's caring for you. He's not _____ _____ _____.

# GROUP DISCUSSION

FOCUS STATEMENT:

**The meaningfulness of our relationship with God is put on display by the flourishing of relationships with others who are also connected to the Vine.**

The way we treat each other is vital to building grace culture. In the same way, grace culture is also built through the way we deal with the pain we've experienced. Sadly, many teens have experienced at least one traumatic event in their life before turning sixteen. According to the Substance Abuse and Mental Health Services Administration, potential traumatic events teens experience include: "psychological, physical, or sexual abuse; community or school violence; witnessing or experiencing domestic violence; national disasters or terrorism; commercial sexual exploitation; sudden or violent loss of a loved one; refugee or war experiences; military family-related stressors (like deployment, parental loss, or injury); physical or sexual assault; neglect; [and] serious accidents or life-threatening illness."[4]

How have you dealt with traumatic experiences to this point in your life?

Trauma affects us emotionally, mentally, physically, and spiritually. The good news is if you have encountered trauma, or even if you haven't, Jesus speaks to both experiences. His Word helps us know how to work together for healing and to prevent passing on trauma to others.

## CONNECTED TO PRODUCE

READ JOHN 15:1-4.

In these verses, Jesus used an analogy to paint a picture of three interwoven relationships. Jesus called Himself the "true vine," which means the vine that has been tested and found to be authentic and genuine. Jesus was tempted but never fell into sin. This means He alone is "true."

The vine is the source of all nutrients to the branch—without being connected to the vine, a branch cannot produce fruit.

Jesus called God the Father "the vinedresser." Another word for vinedresser is farmer, meaning one who is skilled in working the land to produce crops. The vinedresser has a deep interest in the vine and its branches. His expertise and joy allow him to nurture, take care of, prune, and protect the vine and branches. The vinedresser wants to keep the vine and branches in a place where the vine keeps supplying life to the branches so they can bear fruit.

If Jesus is the vine, and God the Father is the vinedresser, who are the branches in this analogy? The answer is simple—we who have embraced Jesus are the branches! I have spent a significant amount of energy in this book to help you realize that God does not cut us out of the family or write us off when we fail. So, does Jesus actually teach this?

Re-read John 15:2. What do you think Jesus meant in this verse?

In this verse Jesus was not saying if we don't bear fruit, God the Father will cut us off from the vine (Jesus). Instead, He was explaining how God the Father will lift or raise us up from an unhealthy place. He will allow us to be washed by God's Word and put on a trellis that helps hold us up so we won't fall back down into a dark place that prevents us from bearing fruit. For us, a trellis He uses to lift us up are things like our student ministry and faith community.

How has God used your faith community to lift you up so that you bear fruit for God's kingdom?

Jesus commands us to keep on abiding in Him. In John's gospel, Jesus used the phrase "abide in me" in two ways. The first sense describes our faith in Jesus when He saved us (see John 6:56). At salvation, we begin to abide in Him. Everyone who has embraced Jesus as their Lord and Savior is already abiding in Him. The second sense describes the intimacy we gain with God through Jesus when we obey His Word (see John 8:31). By hearing God's Word and observing what we hear, we are described as "clean." When we live this way, we keep "abiding" in Christ. When we continue to abide in Christ, we obey His commands (see John 15:10), experience His joy (see John 15:11), love other believers (see John 15:12), and serve as His witness to the world (see John 15:27).

## THE FATHER PRUNES, NOT ABUSES

READ JOHN 15:5-8.

The branches Jesus described here are unique: They're not strong enough to build homes, ladders, or even shelves; they're simply alive to do one thing—bear fruit. If they don't bear fruit, the vinedresser has a choice to make—help it get healthy or remove it. It's important to remember that when Jesus said this to His disciples, He was only hours from His crucifixion. He was telling them these things to comfort them and not cause them fear and anxiety.

When you receive correction from God, do you see it as Him trying to help you get well or something else? Why?

> "I am the vine; you are the branches. Whoever abides in me and I in him, he it is that bears much fruit, for apart from me you can do nothing."
>
> —JOHN 15:5

When God prunes us, His desire is to make us well. God the Father prunes us by calling us to remove people, places, and things from our lives that prevent us from abiding in Jesus. These things keep us from bearing the fruit God the Father has designed for us to bear. When the Father prunes us, it's never abusive; it is always for our good, not for our grief. Abiding in Jesus requires obedience to God's Word. During times we are disobedient, we create tension in our relationship with God, and we don't bear fruit until we confess our sin.

Has there ever been in a time when God called you to remove a person, place, or thing from your life that prevented you from abiding in Jesus? What happened?

In Jesus's day, after the fall harvest when all the fruit had been collected, the vinedresser would look at the bare branches. The vinedresser placed branches that were unproductive and useless in a pile and burned them. This points us to the reality that a day will come when all people will be judged. Those who abide in Christ will bear much fruit. Those who do not abide in Christ will experience a different fate on that day of judgment.

What things in your life are bearing fruit right now? What are things that need to be pruned from your life right now?

## LOVING GOD THE FATHER AND LIVING FOR HIM

READ JOHN 15:9-11

Notice the relationship between God the Father, Jesus, and us. The Father loves Jesus, and Jesus loves us. He told His disciples—and us— to "abide in my love" which is a command, not a suggestion. Jesus demonstrated complete obedience to God the Father because He knows God can be trusted. We then should trust God the Father. Jesus commands us to keep abiding in Him by cooperating with God the Father's pruning process.

How has God proven His love for you most vividly?

Building grace culture includes taking the love God the Father shares with us and sharing it with others. When we do this, we keep the commandment Jesus gave us to obey. When we keep His command, we will experience true joy, and Jesus promises us that our joy will be complete. Remember, we demonstrate our love for God by obeying Him. We will find genuine satisfaction in life when we walk intimately with God. This is the cycle of abiding in Jesus, and these are the benefits and blessings it provides us emotionally, mentally, spiritually, and physically. True satisfaction comes from abiding in Jesus.

What elements of abiding in Jesus bring you the deepest levels of satisfaction?

Take some time to think about the things in your life that give momentary satisfaction but leave you feeling empty. These things harm your fruit-bearing because they prevent you from abiding in Jesus. Consider the items in your life connected to obeying God's commands then fill in the harmful practices in the list below. Think about why you turn to them, and develop an action plan to allow God to prune harmful actions so that you can enjoy more helpful ones.

| Harmful Practices | Why do I keep practicing this? | What helpful practice can replace this harmful one? | How will I work to replace this harmful practice with a helpful one? |
|---|---|---|---|
|  |  |  |  |
|  |  |  |  |

As you close this time of discussion with your group, pray for one another to abide in Jesus. Pray that God would help you learn to allow God to prune you in ways that help you experience the joy of the Lord in your life.

## DAY 1

# GOD THE FATHER IS ACTIVE IN SAVING US

READ 1 PETER 1:3-5.

*Blessed be the God and Father of our Lord Jesus Christ! According to his great mercy, he has caused us to be born again to a living hope through the resurrection of Jesus Christ from the dead, to an inheritance that is imperishable, undefiled, and unfading, kept in heaven for you, who by God's power are being guarded through faith for a salvation ready to be revealed in the last time.*

Over the next three days of personal study, we will take a closer look at how each person of the Trinity interacts with us in love and for our good. Today, we will focus on God the Father. Peter began these verses declaring God the Father to be "blessed." In the original language, this word means to express praise to someone. Peter called his readers to express praise to God because He caused them—and us—to be born again through the resurrection of Jesus.

In ways do you express praise to God the Father?

The phrase "according to" is important. It is opposite of "out of." A way to explain this would be like a billionaire giving a $1 tip at a fancy dinner. He gave "out of" his riches, meaning he took a little bit from what he had and gave it to someone else. The opposite would be a billionaire giving a lavish tip after a fancy meal. This would be "according to" his riches, or a tip that is on the level of the greatness of his wealth. God gives according to His riches, which means when He gives us gifts, He is never stingy!

In what ways has God given to you "according to" the greatness of His love?

God saw us while we were helpless, and according to His "great mercy" (His unlimited reserve of mercy), saved us by causing us to be "born again to a living hope." No one pats themselves on the back for being born. We had nothing to do with being born; we just received the benefit of it. In the same way, we should not praise ourselves for being born again in Christ; we should only praise the One who gave us that life. Through the resurrection of Jesus Christ from the dead, our hope will never die because Jesus is alive.

How does the resurrection of Jesus give you hope?

The word "inheritance" conveys the same idea as the promised land in the Old Testament. However, what God has given His church through the resurrection of Christ is not limited to a piece of land that is not eternal. God has given an inheritance that is: imperishable, undefiled, and unfading. Let's look more closely at what these words mean:

| IMPERISHABLE | it will not die |
| --- | --- |
| UNDEFILED | it will never rot from the inside because it's completely pure and untainted |
| UNFADING | it will never decay or deteriorate |

God the Father is personally guarding us because we have been saved by the resurrection of Jesus. So, today rest in the promises our loving Father has given us that will never be taken away! That's how much God the Father loves you!

Take some time today to reflect on the Father's love. List ways you have seen and know that He loves you. Then, take some time to express your love to Him. Give Him praise from the depths of your heart.

# DAY 2

# GOD THE SON IS ACTIVE IN SUSTAINING US

READ 1 PETER 1:6-9.

*In this you rejoice, though now for a little while, if necessary, you have been grieved by various trials, so that the tested genuineness of your faith—more precious than gold that perishes though it is tested by fire—may be found to result in praise and glory and honor at the revelation of Jesus Christ. Though you have not seen him, you love him. Though you do not now see him, you believe in him and rejoice with joy that is inexpressible and filled with glory, obtaining the outcome of your faith, the salvation of your souls.*

Today we will consider the great work of Jesus in our lives. Although in yesterday's verses Peter explained our future inheritance, he didn't sugar coat the reality that life in the here and now is often filled with grief and various trials. He was comparing what is eternal (our inheritance) with what will expire (our grief and trials).

What struggles or difficult situations have you experienced?

Experiencing grief and trials tests the genuineness of our faith. Through all the years I've walked with Jesus, I've realized life's trials are not for me to prove to God that my faith is authentic. Instead, my faith grows through the difficulties and trials. The struggles we endure are opportunities for our faith to be tested. This is why Peter said our faith is "more precious than gold" (1 Peter 1:7). A tested faith brings praise, glory, and honor to Jesus.

How have you seen your faith grow through struggles and trials?

We must remind ourselves that it takes faith to keep following Jesus, especially when we don't understand what's happening. It takes dedication to follow Jesus because we don't see Him physically and personally with our eyes (see 1 Peter 1:8). This is where faith comes in. Because of the gospel message, we not only believe there was a legitimate historical person named Jesus, but we also believe He is and always has been God. He came in the flesh, lived perfectly, died as a substitute, rose again, ascended to the Father, and will return.

Even though you've never seen Jesus with your eyes, what led you to put your faith in Him?

Hebrews 11:1 defines faith as, "the assurance of things hoped for, the conviction of things not seen." As you walk through your day, consider how Jesus is with you in every difficult situation. The griefs and trials you go through are helping you see that your faith in Jesus is genuine. Be encouraged, God the Father loves you, and God the Son, your Savior, is with you and sustains you as you walk with Him.

Think back across your life and reflect on how faith in Jesus has sustained you through tough days and challenges. Take a moment and thank Him for being there for you and consider how you can help a friend who does not know Him learn more about Him.

# DAY 3

# THE HOLY SPIRIT ACTIVELY SPEAKS TO US

READ 1 PETER 1:10-12

*Concerning this salvation, the prophets who prophesied about the grace that was to be yours searched and inquired carefully, inquiring what person or time the Spirit of Christ in them was indicating when he predicted the sufferings of Christ and the subsequent glories. It was revealed to them that they were serving not themselves but you, in the things that have now been announced to you through those who preached the good news to you by the Holy Spirit sent from heaven, things into which angels long to look.*

On our final day of working to understand God's love in our lives, we come to the Holy Spirit's work. It is helpful for us to remember that the Old Testament prophets were given only part of the complete picture of God's Story. They didn't have all the details we do to see the full picture of the Messiah, who had to suffer but would receive glory.

Although we have the whole story of God today, that does not remove our need for walking by faith (see 2 Cor. 5:7). Not having all the answers to our situations in life can drive us to be more dependent on the Holy Spirit to provide us with the wisdom we need to know how to move forward. The Holy Spirit speaks to us today by convicting us of our sin, reminding us what Scripture says about our lifestyle choices, impressing upon our hearts to do things for God's glory, leading us to help others, giving us understanding when we study Scripture, and in many other ways. We also hear from the Holy Spirit when we're in seasons of suffering. As Jesus endured both suffering and glory, so will we.

When are you most aware of the Holy Spirit's work in your life?

As Christians, we must understand that following Jesus does not prevent us from suffering, though not all suffering is the result of our sinful choices. We live in a fallen world where sin has distorted God's design for life. Christians can suffer from many things like abuse, diseases, the stress of life, and trauma. And, ultimately, we will all face physical death one day (see Heb. 9:27).

How do you feel the presence of the Holy Spirit as you walk through suffering in your life?

One of the ministries of the Holy Spirit is giving us illumination, which is when He shines a light on our hearts and minds and helps us see, understand, and apply God's Word. The Holy Spirit is the One who guided the authors of the Old and New Testaments to write what God shared with them (see 2 Pet. 1:16-21). We can trust all of Scripture!

When has the Holy Spirit spoken to you through God's Word?

Take some time today to consider how angels in God's presence have never received the grace you and I have received. They were not made in God's image like we are. They learn about God's beautiful gift of salvation as they see us live and as they follow God's command to minister to us when necessary. All of this reinforces how much God the Father, the Son, and the Holy Spirit love us. Out of this love, God wants us to grow in our character development and create a culture of grace together.

Take some time to thank God for the work of the Holy Spirit in your life. Consider when He has guided you to right decisions and away from wrong ones. Then close by asking Him to help you know the right direction for your life today.

SESSION SIX

# THE DAY TO DAY

## 2 TIMOTHY 2:22-26

So flee youthful passions and pursue righteousness, faith, love, and peace, along with those who call on the Lord from a pure heart. Have nothing to do with foolish, ignorant controversies; you know that they breed quarrels. And the Lord's servant must not be quarrelsome but kind to everyone, able to teach, patiently enduring evil, correcting his opponents with gentleness. God may perhaps grant them repentance leading to a knowledge of the truth, and they may come to their senses and escape from the snare of the devil, after being captured by him to do his will.

How to live through the day to day with Jesus:

Holding on when life is _____.

Fighting to remain _____ to Jesus.

In our spiritual walk there is no _____-
_____.

If I just hold on to Jesus when life is hard, He will carry me through every single _____.

From the time I wake up, sin is ready to
_____ on me.

> An athlete is not crowned unless he competes according to the rules. It is the hard-working farmer who ought to have the first share of the crops.
>
> — 2 TIMOTHY 2:5-6

Satan uses the same tactics to tempt us that he has _____ used on humanity.

No matter what you face, Jesus will never _____ you.

# GROUP DISCUSSION

FOCUS STATEMENT:

Holding on
when life
is hard and
fighting to
remain faithful
have helped me
to trust God in
every stage of
my life.

Over the last 26 years of walking with Jesus, I have experienced various challenges—some good and exciting and others tragic and sad. I share this to let you know it is possible to love Jesus in your teenage years and to keep growing deeper in your love for Him as you get older. Looking back on my teenage years, I wish someone older would've shared the lessons they learned with me. This is why I have shared this study on grace culture with you.

What is one big lesson you've taken from this study?

Here in the final session, the focus statement is a summary of two things I have practiced in my life. It takes time to bear fruit, so give yourself grace through the seasons of your life. Our journey with Jesus is one where He is writing our story and developing our character along the way. None of us are finished products.

## HOLD ON WHEN LIFE IS HARD

READ 2 TIMOTHY 2:1-13.

Discipleship should be the normal day to day rhythm of life for Christians. In 2 Timothy 2:1-2, Paul challenged Timothy to entrust to others what he had learned from Paul. This reveals how discipleship drives us deeper in our walk with God and friendships with other Christians. Discipleship helps protect us from falling into sin. It helps provide healthy disciplines that give us the spiritual strength we need to walk in victory. As we keep walking in submission to the Holy Spirit, God supplies us with the strength to keep following Jesus.

Who have been the people that you have learned the most from about Jesus? How did they teach you about Him?

Here is how discipleship should work. One maturing believer links his or her life with a less mature believer, and they grow in maturity together for a season. After that season, their relationship doesn't end, but it expands to link their lives with two other people's lives for the next season. Consider this scenario, if each person continues this pattern at the end of four years, 256 people would have walked together in discipleship. This is the impact just one person can make when they begin a reproducible discipleship process in another.

This type of multiplication is what Jesus had in mind when He told His followers to go and make disciples of every ethnicity in Matthew 28:19-20. Imagine what your school could look like if you and four other Christians just made one disciple each semester. The impact would outlive you and me!

Who are four people you could begin this process with? Who could you and your four friends seek to help grow in their walk with Jesus?

In 2 Timothy 2:3-4, Paul used the analogy of a soldier to help us understand how focused disciples of Jesus are to live. Good soldiers keep the orders of the commanding officer as their primary focus; these orders may not be their only focus, but they are the soldiers' most important focus. Our commanding officer is Jesus, who has given us the order to make disciples.

In 2 Timothy 2:5-6, Paul used the example of an athlete to help us understand our walk in Christ. Successful athletes live disciplined lives and see victory because their hard work. In my life, I think about how I was lazy, and during the offseason of wrestling, I would take off from

> Go, therefore, and make disciples of all nations, baptizing them in the name of the Father and of the Son and of the Holy Spirit, teaching them to observe everything I have commanded you. And remember, I am with you always, to the end of the age."
>
> — MATTHEW 28:19-20

working out and watching what I ate. The kids I used to beat easily when I was younger got more challenging for me to defeat as we got older. Since they were more disciplined than I was when we entered high school, I no longer struggled to beat them—they began to beat me!

What areas do you need to focus on to be spiritually disciplined?

For the Jesus follower, there is no off-season because sin never takes a day off. We must be disciplined, not just in our physical lives, but in our spiritual lives. We should be students of the Bible, engage in regular times of prayer, fast when God leads us to, and use the spiritual gifts the Holy Spirit has given us to encourage the faith of other Christians. This is why in 2 Timothy 2:7-8, Paul compared the Christian life to a farmer who puts in work and waits patiently for the harvest when he will see the fruit of his labor. Holding on to Jesus when life gets tough pays off over time.

We must consciously decide to keep holding on to Jesus when life gets tough. Discipleship encourages this reality. Jesus is the perfect example of what it looks like to hold on to God even when loneliness, rejection, and suffering come our way. His life provides a pattern for how to remain close to God even when it seems like He's distant or silent. His resurrection gives His people the strength to know we can endure this intense suffering. Jesus is our living proof that our pain and suffering have an expiration date. This truth gives us the energy to keep holding on when life is hard.

How has discipleship helped you hold on when life is difficult?

## FIGHT TO REMAIN FAITHFUL

READ 2 TIMOTHY 2:14-26.

The second practice that helped me keep following Jesus is fighting to remain faithful to Him alone. There were times in the first few years of my new life in Christ when I was tempted to go back to the worldly pleasures I saw so many of my friends chase. Even my friends in church struggled with the same temptations. The only distinction was that my friends in church were better at hiding their relapses into sin from others. This caused me to consider how my private life naturally bled into my public life. I became motivated to preach what I practiced but also practice what I preached. What we do in private will eventually make its way into the public space, and what we have tried to hide can damage the hearts of others and our witness for Jesus.

In what ways do things done in private become evident in public?

Let's look at 2 Timothy 2:14-26 more closely and see how we can fight to remain faithful. In verse 14, Paul challenged Christians to avoid fighting in public with other people, Christians and non-Christians. This includes group texts, social media, and private conversations. Avoiding public fights will help us learn how to have speech that builds up others instead of tearing them down no matter who's around.

In verse 15, Paul wants us to consider how we talk about God to others. We should know what the Bible teaches and ensure we represent God's truth with as much accuracy and care as possible. We don't want to mislead people by saying things about God that are false or making claims the Bible does not support. Here is a way we can learn how to study the Bible, so we can know what God has said and what He means.

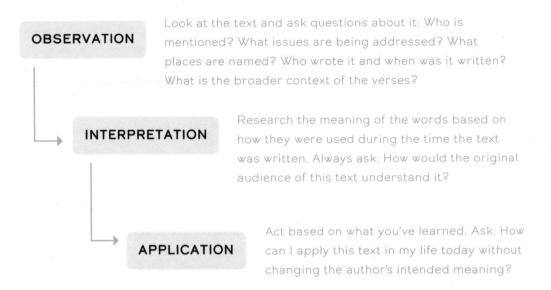

**OBSERVATION**
Look at the text and ask questions about it: Who is mentioned? What issues are being addressed? What places are named? Who wrote it and when was it written? What is the broader context of the verses?

**INTERPRETATION**
Research the meaning of the words based on how they were used during the time the text was written. Always ask: How would the original audience of this text understand it?

**APPLICATION**
Act based on what you've learned. Ask: How can I apply this text in my life today without changing the author's intended meaning?

Lies are tools the evil one uses to distract people away from the truth of God's Word. This is why Satan works so hard to see Christians stop talking about God's Word and talking more about the rumors circling our communities, schools, and even churches. Paul revealed a prime example of this in 2 Timothy 2:17-18. We cannot control how someone else shares what we have told them, therefore our words must always be truthful.

How does being committed to truth telling help you fight to remain faithful?

In 2 Timothy 2:22-26, Paul explained to Timothy some of the most helpful ways to fight to remain faithful. He said to run away from the sinful temptations of youth and run toward righteous, faith, love, and peace. As we run toward these things, we link with others who are pursuing Jesus. Rather than allowing our relationships to be torn apart by petty arguments, part of linking together with other believers means holding our tongues when we're tempted to start or participate in an unnecessary debate. Of course, at times we may need to hear correction from others, and we must receive it with grace. We'll also be used by God to be a voice of correction for other Christians—and grace applies here too. We should use God's Word to correct the wrong behavior with humility, gentleness, and patience.

Which of these ways to remain faithful would be most helpful to you at this point in your life?

It is possible to fall in love with Jesus as a teenager and remain in love with Him decades later—I am living proof. My prayer for you is that you will be focused on making disciples and walking in discipleship relationships. I pray that you will be able to look back at your life years later and say what a blessing it is to love Jesus and help create grace culture. You can do it—I believe in you. But what's even better is that God is with you and will work in and through you as you pursue grace culture.

As you close out this study together, pray for each student to hold on to Jesus when life gets tough and to fight to remain faithful to Him all the days of their lives.

# DAY 1

# SHARE THE WORD

> **READ 2 TIMOTHY 4:1-2.**

*I charge you in the presence of God and of Christ Jesus, who is to judge the living and the dead, and by his appearing and his kingdom: preach the word; be ready in season and out of season; reprove, rebuke, and exhort, with complete patience and teaching.*

Paul's language is heavy here. The word "charge" was used when someone was giving a command to another person standing before witnesses. As we learned from 2 Timothy 2, Paul discipled Timothy and commanded him to do the same for a multi-generational legacy of disciple-making. The witnesses to Paul's charge were "God" and "Christ Jesus." Paul reminded Timothy not only of God and Jesus's awareness of the command that was given but also of the closeness of their presence to those who have been saved. Simply put: Paul was quite serious about Timothy passing on what the apostle had taught him.

What is an important lesson you have learned from a mentor that you have passed along to others? Why is it important to you?

Paul reminded Timothy—and us—that we will stand before God and be evaluated for our obedience throughout our lives. We must realize that as followers of Jesus, we must be ready to share why we follow Jesus to family members, friends, and even strangers. In this way, we are all teachers of God's Word, even if we are not pastors at a church. However, the way we impart His Word to others is very important. We can't approach it casually; our deepest desire must be to accurately convey God's truth to others.

When was a time when you have explained the Bible to someone else? How did you approach the situation?

When God gives us an opportunity to share His Word, we should do three things:

- **Reprove**—to show those in the wrong the error of their belief and behavior

- **Rebuke**—identify by name the lies that are fighting against God's truth

- **Exhort**—encourage those who desire to hear God's Word and apply it, so they will walk in obedience

Which of these three do you find the easiest to do when speaking to others? Which is the hardest?

Make sure you are ready to study God's Word and share it when He calls on you. Always seek to share His Word with patience and grace (see Col. 4:6). How you say something is as important as what you say. If you speak with patience and grace, it's far more likely that others will listen to you than if you are argumentative and angry.

Are you prepared to share God's Word with someone if the opportunity arises? Take some time today and pray about your readiness and the opportunity to speak to someone about Jesus. Remember, you don't have to have all the answers and the Holy Spirit is with you always.

# NOT EVERYONE WANTS TO HEAR TRUTH

READ 2 TIMOTHY 4:3-4.

*For the time is coming when people will not endure sound teaching, but having itching ears they will accumulate for themselves teachers to suit their own passions, and will turn away from listening to the truth and wander off into myths.*

One of the saddest realities I've faced over all the years I've walked with Jesus is when I encounter someone who doesn't want to hear God's truth. It hurts the most is when it is professing Christians who would rather hold on to their views instead of being transformed by the truth of God's Word. Paul prepared Timothy for such encounters.

Have you ever met someone who was unmoved by the truth of God's Word? What happened?

Reading 2 Timothy 4:3-4 makes you believe Paul could see into the future. These verses sound exactly like what's going on today! Paul's day was no different from ours. People filled themselves with the foolish lies of the world around them and didn't developed a hunger for God's truth, just like today. We can fight against this in our own hearts by starving ourselves from the lies of this world to create an appetite for the eternal truth of God's Word.

How have you found God's Word to be superior to what the world offers?

False teaching is everywhere today. People spend countless hours listening to podcasts or watching videos that fill their minds with lies that they begin to believe are valid. It is hard to convince people of their error when they fill their hearts with teachers who are good talkers and make what seem like sound arguments on the surface. However, when we bring what they teach into dialogue with God's Word—which is the whole truth—we will see the holes in the arguments of these false teachers.

Which false teachings do you feel are most prevalent among your circle of friends and acquaintances? How can you lovingly steer them toward the truth?

Sadly, many people don't want to hear God's truth. And, unfortunately, many professing Christians desire to mislead and teach God's Word in a false way. Some seek to twist Scripture to support their own wicked views. Some claim a "new revelation from God" that's only an opinion. For these reasons, we should study Scripture and ask God to examine our hearts and surface the issues He desires to help us work through so we can recognize and eliminate false teaching.

Today read Psalm 139:23-24 and pray these verses to God. Ask Him to search you and bring to light the issues He wants to work with on you so your faith in Him can mature.

# DAY 3

# APPLYING SCRIPTURE

READ 2 TIMOTHY 4:5.

*As for you, always be sober-minded, endure suffering, do the work of an evangelist, fulfill your ministry.*

We need to remember the goal of studying the Bible is not to gain more head knowledge. The purpose of studying the Bible is for us to apply what we have learned. That's what Paul was saying to Timothy in this verse.

Being "sober-minded" is to be aware of false teachings and call them out when we hear them being taught. We must walk in sensitivity to the Holy Spirit when prompted by Him to call out false teachings because if we're not careful, we can become very prideful. It's dangerous to overlook the issues that sit quietly in our own hearts while calling out the issues in others' lives. We need ongoing relationships with people in our church who can help us see the blind spots in our lives that we can't see.

Has anyone ever helped you see a blind spot in your own life? What was it and how did they call it to your attention?

When we are led to call out false teachings, we should expect suffering in some way or another. When we suffer with others, it forms a strong bond in our relationship. Suffering together joins us in closer fellowship with Jesus and each other. Suffering reminds us that our call to follow Jesus was not one He gave just us; His call includes Christians from every ethnicity, both genders, various languages, and locations all across the world.

How have you seen suffering together draw people closer to each other? Closer to Jesus?

Walking in sincere fellowship with other Christians also helps us to be encouraged to do the work of an evangelist, which simply means to share God's story with others. Jesus has saved us so we can share His love with others and they can know His unending love for them. As Paul said in Romans 10:13-15:

> For "everyone who calls on the name of the Lord will be saved." How then will they call on him in whom they have not believed? And how are they to believe in him of whom they have never heard? And how are they to hear without someone preaching? And how are they to preach unless they are sent? As it is written, "How beautiful are the feet of those who preach the good news!"

Do you have beautiful feet? You do if you share the gospel when God provides you the opportunity to do so. So, be a person with beautiful feet. Bringing grace culture to the world around you is a beautiful feet kind of thing to do.

As you close this study, ask God to help you be a bringer of grace culture everywhere you go. Be one who has beautiful feet!

# LEADER HELPS

## SESSION 1

**Leaders Note:** In this session, I frame Scripture as a story God has written. The message of the gospel is the bridge that connects God's story to our individual stories. I help students understand how God has been writing and will continue to write their stories to completion. Lastly, I walk through 1 Corinthians 5:16-21 and help students understand that in Christ you are a new creation.

**Icebreaker:** Play a game of one sentence stories. Go around the group and tell a story. The first person starts with a sentence. The next person adds a new sentence, building off the last sentence or going in a completely new direction. Repeat this until everyone has a chance to add a sentence to the story. Let everyone go twice and see how your one sentence stories twist and turn. Explain that in this session you will talk about the importance of our stories and how God continues to write them.

**Video Answers:** the gospel / image of God / personality, spirituality, morality, rationality / sin / death, unblemished sacrifice / cross / life everlasting / hostility

## SESSION 2

**Leader Note:** In this section, I walk through Luke 6:43-45 and connect it with Galatians 5:19-23 to help students understand how discipleship helps us unlearn our former lifestyle (bad fruit-bearing) and learn how to bear good fruit while walking together with a community that's following Jesus. I also address how Jesus dealt with my sin through discipleship.

**Icebreaker:** Search the internet for real pictures of fruit and fake pictures of fruit. Make the first few obvious, like a blue piece of watermelon or an orange apple. Let students decide which ones are real and which ones are fake. Then discuss how in this session you will learn how to produce real fruit in your life through the process of discipleship.

**Video Answers:** discipleship / accountable / help each other / conclusion / maturity / forgiven / discipleship

# SESSION 3

**Leaders Note:** In this section, I walk through Ephesians 4:25-32. Discipleship deals with our sins, and this gets messy. Relationships in youth groups and life can get tricky. These verses help students learn how to fight their sinfulness on different levels. Knowing this is part of discipleship, we must approach it with realistic expectations. We must understand how to handle conflict in relationships with other Christians and how to view them as opportunities to do better and meet them with grace.

**Icebreaker:** Play a round of two truths and a lie. Direct students to come up with a lie about themselves to pair with two things that are true. Have them share all three and let the other students in the group guess with one is the lie. Lying is one of the many sins the Holy Spirit helps us learn to fight when we walk with Him and in discipleship relationships—even the messy ones!

**Video Answers:** forgiven / speech, selfishness, sinfulness / unpleasing / selfishness

# SESSION 4

**Leaders Note:** In this session, we explore how creating grace culture is in stark contrast to cancel culture. We will compare and contrast cancel culture and grace culture while calling our students who follow Jesus to change the culture of their homes, communities, and schools. Colossians 3:12-15 will serve as the scriptural guide for this discussion.

**Icebreaker:** Gather the supplies to do a 60 second art show. Explain that students must close their eyes and draw a picture within the alloted time, then place their pictures in a pile. Make sure no one signs their pictures or makes any indication of who drew what. Then reveal pictures one at a time. Invite each student to find at least one kind thing about the picture. When everyone has been critiqued, ask, "What could have happened if we'd allowed everyone to truly critique each photo? Why is it so important for us to always speak with grace and kindness—especially when we have to share a tough truth?" In this sessions discussion, we'll see that learning how to address each other with grace and kindness is very important to creating a culture of grace.

**Video Answers:** shaming / forgiveness, mercy, compassion / apart / righteousness / Jesus, each other / boundaries / victory

# SESSION 5

**Leaders Note:** In this session, I walk through John 15:1-11 and touch on the two elements of Jesus's calling to keep abiding in Him. Only when we're connected to Jesus can we produce fruit. And while the word "pruning" might sound hard, we must always remember that the Father prunes us, He doesn't abuse us. Instead, He's trimming away what keeps us from growing spiritually. To produce the fruit the Father calls us to, we must love Him and live for Him. This requires us to abide in Jesus and know that His desire is for us to be well and whole.

**Icebreaker:** Search online for the best "Dad Jokes" available. Recruit three students to stand in front of the group and read the dad jokes and try to make the students laugh. Dad jokes can be corny, but most of them come from a heart of love. We have to carry this understanding when it comes to our heavenly Father. He loves us infinitely, so much that He gave His only Son so that we could live and have a restored relationship with Him. We experience this love when we abide in Jesus and learn firsthand what authentic love looks like.

**Video Answers:** freedom / tough times / Vine / flourishing / power source / consequences, forgiveness / opportunity / mad at you

# SESSION 6

**Leaders Note:** In our final section, I walk students through 2 Timothy 2. I highlight how the practices of holding onto Jesus when life is hard and fighting to remain faithful to Jesus are the two practices I've worked to use each day. Doing these two things has resulted in me walking with Jesus for over twenty-five years. I challenge them to know it's possible to love and live for Jesus for the long haul by assuring them of Jesus's love, care, and desire to carry them along for the rest of their lives.

**Icebreaker:** Instruct students to pair up and give one of the two a blindfold. Then have the one who can see lead the blindfolded student to a goal on the other end of the room. Then, invite the students to switch roles and instruct the blindfolded student to go back to the original starting point, with the partner giving only spoken directions. When the blindfolded students had partners to physically guide them, they still had to hold on to get to the goal. When the blindfolded people only had the voices of their partners, they had to fight to hear one voice over the other voices and noise in the room. This is a perfect illustration of what we'll cover in this session. Note: If students in your group may have negative associations with blindfolds, invite them to close their eyes or cover eyes with their hands.

**Video Answers:** hard, faithful / off-season / storm / pounce / always / abandon

# SOURCES

## SESSION 1

1. Mikkel Wallentin, et al., "Amygdala and heart rate variability responses from listening to emotionally intense parts of a story," *Neurolmage* Volume 58, Issue 3, October 2011, 963-973.

## SESSION 2

2. Chris Aldrich, *The Aldrich Dictionary of Phobias and Other Word Families* (Victoria, Canada: Trafford, 2002), 225.

## SESSION 3

3. K. A. Mathews, *Genesis 1-11:26 Vol. 1A*, (Nashville: Broadman & Holman Publishers, 1996), 174-175.

## SESSION 5

4. Substance Abuse and Mental Health Services Administration, "Understanding Child Trauma," National Child Traumatic Stress Initiative, https://www.samhsa.gov/child-trauma/understanding-child-trauma.

# Get the most from your study.

Promotional videos and other leader materials available at lifeway.com/graceculture.

Many great stories can be traced back to a simple origin. How many first pages reveal the plot twists, conflicts, and experiences that make a book or movie script a true classic in the end?

In each one of us, God is writing a classic tale of belief, redemption, grace, and transformation. It's a story filled with love, but it's not without its share of challenges to overcome. As followers of Jesus, we can expect trials and temptations to challenge our faith and trip us up along the way. Thankfully, Jesus is always present to help us overcome conflicts and persevere through tough times. He teaches us to exchange cancel culture for grace culture. He shows us how to find strength in a community of believers, and He promises to be with us for the long haul.

In this six-session Bible study, author D.A. Horton draws from his life story to show students how God can work through their unique experiences to reveal lives transformed by the love of Jesus.

Lifeway designs trustworthy experiences that fuel ministry. Today, the ministries of Lifeway reach more than 160 countries around the globe. For specific information on Lifeway, visit lifeway.com/students.

## ADDITIONAL RESOURCES

**Grace Culture Video Streaming Bundle**
Six teaching videos from D.A. Horton available at lifeway.com/graceculture.

**Grace Culture eBook**
An eBook format of *Grace Culture*, a six-week study on how we're transformed by the love of Jesus.

Available in the **Lifeway On Demand** app

Stream on these devices: